Escape To Port Isabel

Journal of Winter Texans

By Keith Thorn

© 2025 Keith Thorn. All rights reserved.

This book is a personal travel journal documenting real experiences, places, and events from our journey to Port Isabel and South Padre Island. While the accounts are true to our adventure, some names and details may have been altered for privacy, clarity, or storytelling purposes. Any resemblance to individuals beyond those expressly identified is purely coincidental.

For rights and permissions, please contact:

Keith Thorn
866 Lester Avenue
Collinsville, IL 62234

KeithThorn@KTLLC.net

Published by Amazon KDP

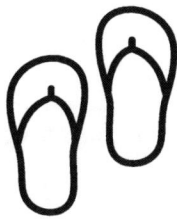

To Melody,
I dedicate this book to us;
we are just livin' the dream one day at a time.
And to our dear friend Joe, who plays pickleball
every day in heaven now.

Foreword

I love to write—poetry, prose, and short stories. I have been writing poetry for at least 60 years and short stories and prose for the past 50. Words don't only convey images; they describe and bring to life emotions and sentiments that might otherwise never come into existence. The written word is a testimonial of what was, what is, or what might be imagined to be.

    Because of my love affair with the magic of words, I read as much as I can, particularly when it can be done in short spurts. This is how I was introduced to the writings that Keith produces. Once I became aware of his literary skills, I followed his collection of works as he progressed and grew—not only as a writer but as a human being. Keith is a man in evolution, journeying forth to become more than he was—to become all that he could possibly be. His is a passage from pain and bondage in his life trials to a new existence, embracing a fresh perspective of joy and enlightenment as he proceeds in his innovative regime of daily living.

    Escape to Port Isabel is Keith's newest effort at bringing forth his insights, feelings, adjustments, and conclusions as he embarks on his latest adventure. Tag along with Keith and his wife, Melody, as they head south to Port Isabel, Texas. Keith is always taking notes—on what he sees, what he feels, and how it all affects him—on his journey to becoming a peaceful man, appreciative of the new experiences he and Melody share. Connect with him as he reflects on each day, often linking his experiences to a song and offering his take on spirituality, forgiveness, and rebirth.

Live through Keith's eyes as he discovers how a man can attach new value to old sights, gain fresh insights from new experiences, and apply life's many lessons to the new standard of living he is establishing for himself. Here, you will meet the martial artist who is finally opening his eyes to see the world anew—relying on past lessons to reshape his way of seeing, creating a new reality through his ventures.

Here is a man, in the middle of his life, who is finally connecting the dots. At last, he understands that the purpose of life is not suffering. Come travel with Keith, and he will show you a different way to perceive even the darkness that might surround you. Watch as he transforms hardships and negative experiences into moments of joy and growth simply by altering his attitude and approach.

This author invites us on his journey of renewal and restoration. Be amazed at how he embraces leisure, play, and meaningful experiences to remold himself into a better man—a more spiritual individual. I see great value in Keith's simple yet practical approach to reinventing himself, recreating the man he always intended to be—the man he should have been had life not thrown him curves.

But life does throw curves. How we adapt to them is the true measure of who we are. Keith has forged a life philosophy, a boldness of style and methodology that allows him to grow within and without, meeting each day with renewed purpose. I am always eager to turn the page and see where his next adventure takes him. Even more so, I am excited to witness his reflections on the life he is now shaping for himself.

Daniel D Johnston

We Ride at Dawn

On Monday morning at -2 degrees, our grand adventure to Port Isabel began with a predawn departure. The morning air was crisp, and as we journeyed onwards, the roads remained clear until we crossed into Arkansas and encountered an unexpected blizzard. With visibility reduced, we navigated the wintry roads at a cautious 30-40 miles per hour for approximately 100 miles.

    A heart-pounding moment occurred when we found ourselves face-to-face with a semi-trailer in our lane, but quick reflexes saved the day, and we safely came to a halt. It appeared the passing cars hadn't given the truck enough space to merge back. Melody snapped a few timely photos, yet we were in shock. We continued, resuming our journey at a more typical 55-60 miles per hour. By 5:30 pm, we reached 18-degree Texarkana, where we activated the propane heater, fired up the electric heater, and settled in for the night. Exhausted from the long day, we easily drifted off to sleep, dogs cared for, and dreams of the road ahead.

Let It Ride

Another early morning start greeted us with a chilly 18-degree dawn in Texarkana, but armed with a positive attitude and, of course, coffee, we embraced the day with a *"Let It Ride"* spirit of *Bachman Turner Overdrive*.

Our journey through North Texas unveiled yet another winter wonderland, complete with a white-knuckle experience for Melody as we encountered icy roads and a brief fishtailing episode while ascending a hill. Thankfully, no oncoming traffic and a swift recovery ensured our safety, even though Melody missed the chance for a perfectly timed photo once again.

After traveling several hundred miles, we finally bid farewell to the last remnants of the snowline as we ventured further into Texas, leaving the blizzard behind us—a welcome sight indeed.

Navigating Houston was a breeze, thanks to a trusty co-pilot and an in-car photographer. Although we passed through Houston, we decided to call it a night at an RV campground initially named El Campo. However, after circling the highway underpass a couple of times without success, we continued onto Ganado, TX, where we found a cozy, albeit small, RV park—a perfect spot to spend the night.

Given the frigid temperatures, we opted not to hook up to water or de-winterize just yet, as another chilly night with lows around 20 degrees awaited us.

'Would you let it ride?
Would you let it ride?
Would you let it ride?
Yeah-yeah, would you let it ride?'

You Gotta Love It

Wednesday got off to an early start in the pre-dawn dark, but there was a twist—I was only half awake when I drove off without connecting the camper's power line to the truck and forgot to unplug from the campground's electric source. It wasn't until we stopped at an exit that Melody asked about the trailer plug, and a quick look in the rear-view mirror revealed that the camper's lights were off, and the electric line was trailing alongside the travel trailer. In my haste to move, I had inadvertently ripped it out of the connection. Talk about a wake-up call!

It's moments like these that never fail to amaze me with the occasional lapses in judgment. I always say that I've just added another story to my list of 'dumb ass' moments when offering advice.

We continued down the road and reached the first McDonald's at 7:15 AM, only to find it still closed. After a 15-minute wait and another 15-minute delay in getting our order, we couldn't help but feel the frustration of lost time during those moments as the food tasted like yesterday's leftovers warmed, but hardened*

The wind farms in Texas are a sight to behold, stretching over vast areas that seem to be at least five to ten miles square. Interestingly, about 20% of the turbines were not in operation, a reminder of the challenges posed by the freezing conditions that have affected the Midwest, including Texas, this year.

As we ventured further into South Texas, the landscape transformed into rugged terrain adorned with cacti, scraggly trees, and shrubs along the flat prairies. It wasn't until we were approximately 100 miles from Port Isabel that everything turned lush and green, with palm trees dotting the scenery. We finally arrived in Port Isabel around 1 PM and spent the next three hours checking in, giving the truck and camper a thorough wash, and commencing the setup process for electric, water, and sewage. Tomorrow, we plan to head over to the nearby beach, but first, we need to stock up on propane, replace a defective propane hose, and get a new light cap for the trailer exterior—apparently, the cold had blown it off during our travels.

We're truly grateful for the kind words and support we've received every day of this journey, and we hope you're as excited about the adventures of this year as we are!

Windows Open or Closed

Every day begins with a comical wake-up call from our dogs, who seem to have mastered the art of bad sleep manners. The truth is, I'm usually up by 5 AM, and the dogs can't contain their excitement for the morning routine—breakfast, walks, and the essential business of pooping before settling back into slumber. Melody is pleased when we are done, dogs back asleep, and me working away at the computer ...

Thursday was a flurry of activity as we continue to fine-tune our setup. Melody set-up and created a new cooking area, set up an enclosed day tent, and reorganized the travel trailer for maximum comfort. The community here offers a convenient propane service—$20 fills up our tanks, ensuring we're well-prepared for the days ahead. I spent some time replacing a propane hose that had gone bad and obstructed the gas flow, though we might not need the heater for the rest of the year, the hot water heater still relies on propane.

We took a leisurely stroll with the dogs around the gated community today to acquaint ourselves with its offerings—docks, the dog park, heated hot tub and swimming pool, community center, showers, and much more.

We ate a quick sandwich made from some lunch meat we had on hand, and I indulged in a beer and sun-soaked nap, earning a subtle burn on my face as a souvenir.

Later in the day, we embarked on a series of errands, making stops at Walmart, the RV Center, and a delightful dining spot called White Sands on the waterfront. The food was delicious, the prices were reasonable, and the atmosphere was refreshingly unpretentious—a perfect match for our personal taste.

With showers taken and bedtime approaching, we're treated to a stunning view of the evening sun. Tonight, we've decided to keep the travel trailer windows open, embracing the calm and comfortable 55-degree night.

Morning Blessings

In the early pre-dawn hours, the dogs and I complete our morning routine, a symphony of chores that Melody cherishes for the serene silence it offers. As I delve into coffee and organizing web workloads for the morning, this has become our cherished ritual.

Today, we embarked on a quest to tackle more errands, which led us to Brownsville in pursuit of a router and cable setup for the upcoming nine weeks. We also made a pit stop at the local shoe repair shop in San Benito to drop off Melody's new cowgirl boots for stretching, ensuring a more comfortable fit. (We'll return next Wednesday to collect them.) Additionally, we stocked up on more RV parts and indulged in a delectable taco feast at El Ray Del Taco restaurant.

While driving along Highway 100 back to Port Isabel, we passed a collection of bronze bull smokers for sale, their phone number prominently displayed for any potential buyers*

One remarkable aspect of our time here has been encountering fellow travelers from the Northwest and Northern states like Washington, Minnesota, and Michigan. No matter what brings them to this part of the world, they all share a common appreciation for the warmth and charm found here.

The Rain in Spain

The rain has been our steadfast companion since yesterday, and it shows no signs of letting up today. Yesterday morning was consumed by the task of setting up the Spectrum WiFi, modem, and router, with a minor hiccup involving the outside cable line being too short—something that required some troubleshooting. The rest of the day was dedicated to organization, intermittent naps, and hearty meals, all accompanied by final episodes of 'Reacher' before we retired to bed.

Each morning, well before dawn, I embark on a tranquil walk down to the marina with the dogs. On weekdays, the fishing boats gather and make their way to the bay, but weekends are a different story. This Sunday morning, as the rain gently pattered on the water, I captured a photo of the serene scene that unfolded before me—a moment of quiet beauty.

But, as it often goes, our morning began with a touch of drama. Startled by the rain, Cardi, one of our dogs, bolted while I was taking this photo on the pier. She dashed towards our travel trailer, which was about 400 yards away in the dim morning light. Bella, our blind companion, required my assistance as I carried her back to safety.

Afterward, I set out to find Cardi, who had veered off the direct path to the camper and was about 50 yards away. In the hushed pre-dawn stillness, she wasn't hard to locate, being the only moving presence in the area. We are fortunate to be in a gated community, which ensured our wet and muddy canine friend made it back home safe and sound.

Rainy Days and Mondays

Our unused cooking area stands as a reminder of the continuous rain that has persisted for the past three days, keeping us from enjoying it as planned. Our culinary repertoire has adapted to the weather with soups, sandwiches, chips, and cookies serving as our rainy-day menu.

Sunday unfolded in a rather tranquil manner. After tending to the dogs' needs, I typically dive into my daily ritual of catching up on emails and managing web work orders—a routine that extends throughout the week, without pause. Some days, like this morning work may be brief, while others see me engaged with it on and off, spanning from morning to evening, all contingent upon our clients' requirements.

I also tackled some minor repairs that were overdue, like addressing a bathroom sink discoloration issue (peroxide, baking soda, and UV) and reinforcing the entry door screen with an additional dog protector for added security, especially important since Bella is blind, and the screen alone wouldn't suffice.

Melody, on the other hand, hadn't utilized her Mac Book Air in nearly a week, as she relied on her iPad and iPhone (yes, we embarked on our journey from St. Louis last Monday at dawn). When she attempted to log in, she encountered persistent login issues that led to lock-out and frustration. Hours passed as she grappled with this obstacle. I tried various solutions. Eventually, she resorted to restarting the OS and utilizing the 'keyboard did not work' setting to reset the login password, bringing things back to normal. Funny how this setting blames the keyboard for the wrong entry.

This rainy day ended up being filled with myriad minor tasks that collectively transformed it into a full day of activity.

Typically, I attempt to draft the beginnings of these morning posts the night before, but around 4 o'clock, I headed for a shower and accidentally cut my finger on a razor that was placed on the shower tray. Strangely, it didn't hurt much, but the bleeding wouldn't cease long enough for me to assess the wound. I went through an entire roll of toilet paper in the span of 15 minutes, wrapping layers that were two inches thick or more.

Thankfully, Nurse Melody came to my rescue, and for an additional 10+ minutes, we worked together to staunch the bleeding. After exhausting the resources of a first blood-soaked gauze bandage, she applied a second one that finally did the trick. We realized it wasn't as much a cut as it was a small gash on the top third of my finger.

After a medicinal sip or two, I called it a night, hoping that the rain that persisted today and Monday would finally relent, granting us a glimpse of sunshine once more.

Just One Day

Our Monday included a familiar visit to 'Wally World' which seems like a part of our daily morning ritual as we needed an assortment of supplies. On the list were various food items, a six-plug adapter for outlets, a squeegee for the outside windows—much needed after three days of rain—and, finally, essentials like *BleedStop*, waterproof tape, and butterfly band-aids. Remarkably, when we removed the bandage from the previous night, it seemed like I possessed an abundance of vitamin K and boasted impressive healing capabilities!

Laundry day turned into a rigorous workout for Melody, who soon discovered that lugging loads of laundry to and from the washer and dryers was no walk in the park. She effortlessly racked up 5,000 steps today, complete with an added strength-training, anaerobic workout for good measure*

We continued to enhance our campsite setup after the days of rain by attaching 'noodles' to the ground support lines of the Coleman screened-in canopy. This safety measure is designed to prevent accidental collisions with these lines, which can be a hazard at night, especially for unsuspecting visitors who may not see or remember them.

Our dogs reveled in their walk around the area and cherished a visit to their special, gated dog park. No leashes, just run and fun as the air was filled with information about potential new canine friends. An added convenience of the park was the availability of poop bags and trash cans. Although many people here have dogs, the park remains astonishingly clean, as everyone conscientiously picked up after their furry companions.

What a transformation just one day can bring. With the help of beautiful sunshine and temperatures reaching 70 degrees, we engaged in an outdoor cleanup and organization session. The Food Court officially opened, much to our delight! The ice machine churned out ice cubes as we collected them for a few hours to stock our cooler. However, the Margaritaville section remained closed during today's lunch rush.

Our culinary adventure on the Blackstone grill on Monday featured: Butter-cooked large shrimp, Portabella mushrooms, and tangy rice—a delightful mini-feast. This culinary delight was followed by a well-deserved nap, bathed in the warm sunshine.

Play Misty for Me

Living in a tiny home is a captivating journey where everything assumes larger-than-life significance. Whether it's a slightly ajar cabinet door, unfolded clothes, an open food container, last night's unwashed dishes, or our dogs playfully sprawled in the floor's path, these and most ordinary moments can swiftly transform into clutter, disarray, and a pervasive sense of disquiet. Within the snug confines of our small space, my admiration for my wife, Melody, and I, along with our two beloved dogs, has deepened as we've gleaned profound insights about ourselves. Along this path, we've come to discern that certain things simply pale in significance, while others bear substantial weight. Our shared aspiration revolves around consistently discovering the silver linings, harmonizing the delicate equilibrium, and nurturing each other's well-being—an enduring odyssey in pursuit of contentment.

Tuesday morning, I embarked on a quest of my own, in search of a local hardware store to improve the hanging space for our clothes, just a few blocks from our home. I stumbled upon an old-fashioned local hardware store called White Lumber and Supply. Unlisted on Google, yet this place is a treasure trove of useful items. The helpful store attendant greeted me warmly, and I sketched my design ideas to reinforce our closet's strength. We engaged in a few rounds of brainstorming, with his insight of possibilities and revisions refining my concept. In no time, I had all the necessary materials and pre-cut wood for my project, and it only set me back $18! Upon returning, Melody and I began the mad scientist process of turning my idea into reality, and presto—it worked!

    Today, we ventured to the pool for the first time since our arrival. Despite the inviting 70-degree weather, the overcast skies and misty conditions made it feel more like hot tub weather. Please don't be alarmed by my description of the scene at the hot tub; while one gentleman may have had a striking appearance, he was simply another guest enjoying the soothing waters.

    Before heading to the pool, we took the dogs on a brisk walk to tire them out, ensuring their comfort in their large crates while we were away. In the rear section of our travel trailer, we've replaced the bedding in the bunks with carpet, making it a cozy space for our furry companions.

    We crossed the nearby bridge to South Padre Island, a sprawling and captivating destination. The lengthy bridge spans light-green, shallow waters, creating an otherworldly atmosphere with the misty or foggy weather. We explored the area, including the Visitor Center, where we picked up brochures, notably one for the Metro Bus Transit, which operates regularly. In preparation for Matt and Carol's visit in February, we stopped by the Palms Resort to establish a connection and gather information about where their accommodations would be.

On our way back, we were overwhelmed by the multitude of dining options on the island. Ultimately, we decided to return to our home base and dine at a nearby establishment we really like the one called 'White Sands', only to discover it was closed on Mondays and Tuesdays. It was a friendly reminder that cooking at home is a wonderful alternative on those days. We meandered back to the Port Isabel Lighthouse area, exploring the artsy neighborhood and strolling a few blocks off the main street. Our quest for an unpretentious dining experience led us to Joe's Oyster Bar. The food was quite satisfying! We concluded our meal with full stomachs and made it back for a two-hour siesta as I lay there pondering why I don't know the lyrics to 'Misty'.

Embracing the Sound of Silence

In a world that's perpetually buzzing with noise, there's a certain enchantment in the quiet of the early morning hours. As the first rays of sunlight gently caress the horizon, I find myself drawn to the symphony of silence that envelops our lives. It's a unique experience—one that resonates deeply with my soul.

The mornings here are unlike any other. There's a tranquility that reigns, broken only by the soft padding of paws as our two beloved dogs make their way to the door, eager to greet the new day. Their enthusiasm is infectious, yet it doesn't disrupt the serene ambiance that lingers in the air.

I step outside, taking a moment to savor the crispness of the morning air. The world is still asleep, wrapped in a blanket of quietude. All around me, nature seems to hold its breath, as if in anticipation of the day ahead. The only sound I hear is the gentle lapping of water against the marina's edge.

I walk down to the marina, where the fishing boats stand in stoic silence, their reflections mirroring in the tranquil waters. It's a scene that never fails to captivate me—the perfect alignment of these vessels, as if they, too, are paying homage to the peacefulness of the dawn.

With my camera in hand, I capture this moment of serenity, knowing that the photo will serve as a reminder of the beauty that resides in the sound of silence. The lines of fishing boats stand as sentinels of tranquility, guardians of a world untouched by the clamor of everyday life.

As the sun continues its ascent, the world gradually awakens. The symphony of silence gives way to the hum of daily activities. But for those precious moments at sunrise, I find solace in the quietude, in the sound of silence that speaks volumes to my soul.

In a world that rarely pauses to catch its breath, I've come to appreciate the mornings here, where the sound of silence reigns supreme, and where the world seems to hold its collective breath, allowing me to bask in the serene beauty of a new day.

Here Comes the Sun

At 3 am I was up and later welcomed the still dark morning's arrival, filled with thoughts of gratitude that kept sleep at bay. Melody knows that when my mind brims with something to share, sleep eludes me.

More than eight days had passed since we last basked in the warmth of the sun's embrace, and the longing for its radiant presence had grown insatiable. Our journey began on January 15th, departing Collinsville in the early hours with the mercury hovering at minus 2 degrees. While the temperatures had gradually risen after the initial bone-chilling days, South Texas had greeted us with more rain than rays.

But then came Thursday, a day that unveiled the full splendor of Port Isabel—a beautiful, sunny canvas painted against the backdrop of 70-degree weather. It was nothing short of spectacular.

In our daily routines, we strike a balance between discipline and flexibility, allowing ourselves a few hours of leeway between the wants, the needs, and the desires. Our canine companions, always eager to explore the outdoors, can impose their own schedule on our lives. Yet as I lay awake, unable to sleep, my heart brimmed with gratitude.

Another day of sunshine awaited us, and I couldn't help but wish the same warmth and radiance for your heart, mind, and soul.

You Were Always on My Mind

As our 80-day adventure unfolds, Melody and I find ourselves riding the waves of excitement and the roller coaster of fun that comes with exploring new horizons. What has truly amazed us on this journey is the outpouring of love and support from our friends and family, who have been inspired by our quest for adventure and self-discovery.

Friday as the sun graced us with its warm embrace, we decided to take a leisurely dip in the heated pool. The temperature soared close to 75 degrees, creating the perfect backdrop for our tranquil afternoon. But what truly made this day special was the wonderful company we enjoyed with each other—the kind that leaves a lasting impression.

Amid our relaxing day, I received a phone call from a dear friend living in Dallas, Kevin. His success story is nothing short of remarkable. Kevin is not only one of the most accomplished individuals I know in leadership, but he's also someone I deeply respect for his unwavering faith, dedication, and achievement. It was a humbling moment when Kevin shared with me that Melody and I inspire him.

Kevin's call served as a powerful reminder that our lives and the choices we make have the potential to impact others in ways we may not always realize. People are watching us, and our actions can serve as a source of inspiration. His words encouraged us to keep striving for happiness, to savor every moment, and to uplift and support those around us.

So, to Kevin and everyone who has shared in our journey, we want you to know that you were always on our minds. Your encouragement fuels our spirits and motivates us to be the best versions of ourselves. May we all continue to inspire one another, finding joy in the simple act of living, and creating ripples of positivity that touch the lives of those we encounter.

Thank you, Kevin, for reminding us of the profound impact we can have on others by simply embracing life with open arms and open hearts.

Unforeseen Challenges

Late Friday afternoon, we received an unexpected call from our thoughtful neighbors. Their message delivered news that Ameren utility trucks were parked in front of our home, and their purpose was anything but reassuring. It appeared that a widespread electric outage further down our cul-de-sac had prompted Ameren to act, and this meant some significant digging right in our front lawn.

As we gazed at the scene unfolding before us, a whirlwind of thoughts raced through my mind. The culmination of three years of hard work and meticulous lawn maintenance suddenly felt jeopardized. It wasn't the first time we found ourselves in this predicament, as companies like AT&T had previously undertaken similar endeavors, leaving the underground electric fence damaged and my pleas for repairs unanswered.

In moments like these, it's easy to succumb to frustration and despair, feeling as though all our efforts had been in vain. But life often presents us with challenges, and it's our response to them that truly matters. Instead of dwelling on the inconvenience, we chose to see this as an opportunity—an opportunity to transform a problem into a solution.

While the situation was far from ideal, it also served as a reminder of our ability to adapt and overcome obstacles. After all, there's a saying that goes, "There's a problem for every solution." In this case, we are determined to find that solution and ensure that our home remained the sanctuary we have worked so hard to cultivate.

What A Wonderful World

Saturday morning greeted me as usual, half-awake and fumbling in the dark to feed the dogs by lantern light. I reached for what I thought was my tea, only to realize I'd taken a swig of Kikkoman Soy Sauce! Laughter ensued, a wild start to our day.

Our RV Park in Port Isabel held a community-wide garage sale, a treasure trove of RV folks' extra stuff. We strolled through the sale, finding a few gems and enjoying meeting fellow travelers. A soda truck offered fun drinks, and one family even served a free breakfast of pancakes, eggs, sausage, and bacon, a gesture to connect with the community. This place has become a home away from home for many, and we felt the warmth of camaraderie.

In the afternoon, we basked in the sun, recharging like batteries in the warmth, even the dogs seem to enjoy while often lying face-up. Evening found us back at White Sands for dinner, savoring 1/2 Off Happy Hour, new appetizers like Loaded Texas Fries and Bacon-Wrapped Jalapeño Shrimp (minus the jalapeños). As the day ended, we couldn't help but be grateful, recognizing that Melody and I are living our dreams together in this wonderful world.

Just Let Them

Today my mind wanders to the poignant verses of Cassie Phillips' poem, "Just Let Them" (the tattoo is also on my right hand). As I wander along this beautiful place, the poem's words resonate within me: "Just let them."

In this tranquil town, each sunrise over the Gulf of Mexico is a testament to the natural wonders that envelop us, urging both my wife Melody and me to treasure every fleeting moment. The vibrant colors of dawn paint the sky with hope, inspiring us to embrace life's transitory joys.

Phillips' poem encourages us to let others make their choices, to let them be who they are, and to let them show us their true selves. Here, in this idyllic setting, we've discovered the power of letting go. Whether we're watching the sun dip below the horizon, reflecting on the tide's ebb and flow, or simply enjoying the company of newfound friends, we've learned to release our grip on expectations and judgments.

"Let them lose you," the poem advises. In Port Isabel, we are learning to appreciate the unique rhythms of life here, to savor every interaction and experience, no matter how brief or ordinary.

The poem implores us to "let them love you." In this coastal haven, we've opened ourselves to the warmth and kindness of the people who call this place home for months at this time of the year. Their genuine hospitality has touched our hearts, reminding us of the beauty of human connection.

As we reflect on our journey in Port Isabel, we see how the wisdom of Phillips' poem has woven itself into our experiences. We are learning to let go, to embrace the beauty of the present moment, and to allow the world to reveal itself in its own time. This coastal sanctuary has become a place of transformation, where we've discovered the power of surrender and the joy of embracing life's ever-changing tides.

I'm A Rich Man

In the heart of Port Isabel, where the sun kisses the sea each morning, my wife Melody and I have embarked on an 80-day journey filled with introspection, chaos, serenity, and unexpected lessons. The tranquil beauty of this coastal haven has allowed us to explore the depths of our thoughts and emotions, much like the verses of the song "I'm a Rich Man" by Little Big Town, which seem to echo in the gentle breeze that sweeps through this whole experience.

As I stroll along, the lyrics of the song resound in my mind: "I'm a rich man, better than blessed man, Had all I ever wanted, I got everything I need, Got love and a family" In this idyllic setting, every sunrise over the Gulf of Mexico becomes a testament to the wealth that surrounds us, a reminder to cherish each moment. The vibrant hues of dawn paint the sky with hope, inspiring us to embrace life's fleeting joys.

"I ain't lookin' for a pot of gold, That ain't what this life means to me, I keep my head up high, feet on the ground, Love the ones I'm living 'round, Life is just that simple to me" the song continues. In Port Isabel, I'm reminded that true wealth lies not in material possessions but in the bonds, we share with loved ones. Whether it's a conversation with a fellow traveler, the laughter of people

playing, or the gentle rustling of palm leaves in the breeze, these moments, like the song suggests, are the true treasures of life.

The song also celebrates the simplicity of love: "I keep my head up high, feet on the ground, Love the ones I'm livin' 'round, Life is just that simple to me" In this coastal sanctuary, my wife Melody and I have discussed that our journey together is the greatest gift of all. We've learned to appreciate the beauty of existence and to embrace life's fleeting moments with gratitude and love.

As I reflect on our experiences after almost two weeks in Port Isabel, I'm reminded of the song's closing lines: *"A better than blessed man, Had all I ever wanted, I got everything I need, I got everything I need, Got love and a family"* In this coastal haven, we've found richness beyond measure in each other's company, in the simple pleasures of life, and in the joy of embracing the journey.

Cardi's Transformation

Meet Cardi, our beloved Lab, Heinze 57 mix who entered our lives about five years ago after being rescued from the woods alongside her brother. From the very beginning, Cardi has been a bit "skittish" when confronted with the unknown, often displaying craziness when new elements entered her environment.

However, the past two weeks have marked a significant turning point for Cardi. It's remarkable how much difference constant exposure to other animals and people can make. With dogs passing by and various activities happening around her, Cardi is slowly but surely becoming more at ease and acclimated to her surroundings.

Cardi has always been the type of dog who gazes out the window and barks at anything and everything. But now, we're witnessing a shift as she begins to trust that all is well and there's no need for her to be overly protective or reactive unless we signal a genuine threat. Thankfully, we haven't had to do that so far. We have faith that animals have a keen sense of danger and respond accordingly when needed.

Our daily routine involves taking Cardi and her furry companion Bella for multiple walks throughout the day and spending countless hours outdoors with them. While they may have grown somewhat bored with the activity of other people and animals now, we remain optimistic that in a few months, Cardi will continue her journey of transformation, becoming a more confident and comfortable dog in all kinds of environments.

    As we sit outside, soaking up the sunshine and listening to the music on the Echo, we can't help but appreciate these moments of tranquility with our faithful companions. Bella, our small Jack Russell, Chihuahua mix, may be old and blind, but she revels in the warmth of the sun and good music, reminding us to savor those simple joys of life.

The Boot-Scootin' Boogie

Before stepping onto Texan soil, we were well-aware that our wardrobe was missing an essential piece: boots. So, we embarked on a mission to find the perfect pairs of boots that would not only serve us well but also allow us to immerse ourselves in the Texan spirit. We each acquired a pair of meticulously crafted boots, made in Mexico, as we prepared for an exciting adventure – our first visit to a real rodeo!

Mark your calendars for the 3rd weekend in February, because that's when the local rodeo rolls into town, just a short 17-mile drive down highway 100. What makes it even more exhilarating is that this rodeo is a 'qualifying' event, promising an authentic and thrilling experience that we've never encountered before. Melody can hardly contain our excitement, eager to witness the breathtaking displays of skill and bravery that define rodeo culture.

But that's not all; we're also looking forward to embracing the Texan nightlife. Melody and I are planning some unforgettable date nights that involve boot-scootin' and dancing to the irresistible rhythms of Texas country music. While I might not have the smoothest dance moves,

I'm prepared to give it my all and take on those 'slides' with enthusiasm.

So, keep us in your thoughts and prayers as we hit the dance floor, ready to enjoy an activity that I might not excel at but am more than willing to embrace. Perhaps a few beverages will help my boots find the right rhythm on the dance floor!

Yeah, heel toe, docie doe, come on, baby, let's go, boot scootin'
Oh, Cadillac, Black Jack, baby meet me outback we're gonna boogie
Oh, get down turn around go to town boot scootin' boogie

Never Been to Spain

Over the past two+ weeks, my wife Melody and I have embarked on a remarkable journey filled with new experiences, introspection, chaos, and an abundance of cherished moments.

Our destination, Port Isabel, has been a coastal haven that has not only allowed us to explore the depths of our thoughts and emotions but has also introduced us to the warm embrace of its community. As we hang out in this beautiful place, the lyrics of the song "Never Been to Spain" resonate within me, weaving our adventures into a fairy tale of discovery and togetherness.

The quaint town of Port Isabel, where the sun graces us with its presence each morning, has become a canvas of wonder. "Never been to Spain, but I kinda like the music," the song's lyrics echo in my mind as I stroll along the community here and every sunrise over the Gulf of Mexico becomes a testament to the natural beauty that surrounds us, inspiring us to savor each moment.

As we've settled into this coastal sanctuary, I'm reminded of the song's sentiments: "Well, I've never been to heaven, but I've been to Oklahoma." While Port Isabel may not be heaven, it certainly feels close to it. The warmth of the locals, the stunning scenery, and the simplicity of life here have given us a taste of paradise. We've explored the local culture, forged new connections, and indulged in the simple pleasures of existence.

"Never been to Spain, but I kinda like the music." In Port Isabel, we've discovered the universal language of happiness and contentment. Whether we're enjoying the vibrant melodies of life or basking in the sun's gentle rays, we've found that true richness lies in the moments we share and the bonds we nurture. Our journey has become a blend of exploration, reflection, and the joy of togetherness, echoing the spirit of "Never Been to Spain."

'Well, I never been to Spain
But I kinda like the music
Say the ladies are insane there
And they sure know how to use it
They don't abuse it
Never gonna lose it
I can't refuse it, mhm'

Your Song

Friday brought overcast skies and a persistent breeze that prompted us to tackle multiple shopping errands and tiny home improvement projects, including the installation of new shelves in our clothing storage area.

One lesson we've learned today is to avoid Wally World on Fridays in the Port Isabel area. It felt like the entire town decided it was free appetizer day as shoppers crowded the food aisles, preparing for their weekend meals.

As the day progressed, the overcast skies provided the perfect backdrop for a cozy evening. The scene captures the late-day ambiance, with Melody deeply immersed in a book she had started earlier and finally finished. At home, her personal library holds nearly 700 books—a true reflection of her love for reading. Witnessing her contentment and relaxation in this tranquil setting is a joy.

It's moments like these that remind me of the beautiful sentiment expressed in Elton John's "*Your Song*," as I can't help but think, "This is your song, my sweet lady."

'And you can tell everybody
This is your song
It may be quite simple, but now that it's done
I hope you don't mind, I hope you don't mind
That I put down in words
How wonderful life is
While you're in the world'

Ol' St Lou

Saturday morning, we embarked on a crazy (for me) adventure to a local church rummage sale, and it turned out to be quite a successful shopping spree. We managed to snag 21 items for a mere $11, a testament to our great partnership in finding amazing additions for our tiny home and some fun clothing items like a Panama hat for me.

Our journey then took us to the island, where we paid a visit to the Palms Resort. Our friends Ron and Lauren from 'The Lou', who have been enjoying their stay there since December, welcomed us with beautiful smiles. (Matt and Carol are coming here also in February) After a fantastic Red Snapper lunch at the Palms Resort Cafe on the Beach, we shared stories and caught up on each other's lives.

On our way back to Port Isabel, we encountered an unfortunate accident that caused a 30-minute delay in island traffic. Despite the minor setback, we returned home just in time to bask in the sun's warm embrace for a few hours before Melody prepared a delicious soft taco dinner.

Here in Port Isabel and South Padre Island, I've noticed that many people hail from northern states like Michigan, Minnesota, North Dakota, and beyond. When folks ask where we're from, I proudly sport my 'The LOU' hat, which often piques their curiosity about our hometown.

Instead of simply saying 'Illinois,' I prefer to evoke the spirit of 'The LOU' (St. Louis), as boldly proclaimed by my black hat.

As my friend Pat Liston expressed in the St Louis Mama's Pride classic, *"Ol St Lou"*:

'So, if you wanna see the birth of the blues,
Come on to Ol' St. Lou
Yeah, it's the one and only place
Where they can lay it down for you'

It's A Beautiful Morning

As the day broke, Melody and I found ourselves wrapped in the gentle embrace of a new morning in Port Isabel. This time, it was Melody who initiated our day with the timeless tune, "*It's A Beautiful Morning.*" It brought a smile to my face, for this song holds a special place in our morning routine back home. It was heartwarming to witness Melody starting her day with this cheerful melody.

Sunday unfolded like any perfect Sunday should, at 75 degrees and us basking under the sun's warm rays from morning till around three in the afternoon, our spirits soaring. Our time at the pool led to pleasant encounters with fellow travelers who have returned here numerous times. Their stories painted a vivid picture of the wonders that surround us, from the last Civil War battlefields (fought even after the war officially ended) to the Space-X facilities across from Brownsville, the turtle sanctuary, wildlife sanctuaries on South Padre Island, and the inviting, best drive-on beaches.

Yes, the South Texas sun is relentless, and we feel its intensity from the early hours. But it truly was a beautiful morning, and we're reminded of the Young Rascals' lyrics.

Indeed, each new day in Port Isabel is a precious gift, an opportunity to explore, create memories, and savor the beauty of life with Melody.

'It's a beautiful morning, ah
I think I'll go outside for a while and just smile
Just take in some clean fresh air, boy
(Ain't) no sense in staying inside
If the weather's fine and you got the time
It's your chance to wake up and plan another brand-new day'

My Girl

Monday morning brought us to the campground meeting where they outlined all the activities for the week. Swimming pool workouts, upcoming tours, indoor games, outdoor games, crafts, potlucks, and more were all on the agenda. It was a delightful blend of fun and information, setting the tone for our week ahead.

Despite the gusty winds, and and temperatures reaching a sunny 65 degrees, we had to make a change of plans for dinner. Cooking outside was initially the idea, but the winds had other ideas, and so we opted for the air fryer to prepare a delicious meal of salmon and wild rice.

As we reflect on our first three weeks here in Port Isabel, the lyrics of "My Girl" come to mind:

I've got so much honey The bees envy me

Indeed, our time here has been sweet, filled with the simple joys of life, laughter, and new experiences. Just like the song says, there's something special that can make us feel this way, and it's the beauty of our surroundings, the warmth of newfound friendships, and the adventure that unfolds each day. Port Isabel has become our own little slice of paradise, and we're cherishing every moment together.

'I don't need no money, fortune, or fame
I've got all the riches baby one man can claim
Well I guess you'd say
What can make me feel this way
My girl, my girl, my girl'

Don't Let the Old Man In

I found myself reflecting on the profound words of Toby Keith's song, "Don't Let the Old Man In," on Tuesday morning. Despite already posting for the early morning, the song's poignant message lingered, resonating deeply as we navigate our days in the serene haven of Port Isabel, where the sun and sea seem to hold the secrets of eternal youth. Toby Keith's wisdom serves as a poignant reminder that life is fleeting, urging us to seize every moment.

In our cozy tiny home nestled amidst the tranquility of Port Isabel, I couldn't help but ponder the significance of these lyrics. It's all too easy to slip into routines, to become complacent, and to let the passage of time take its toll. Yet, the song's message empowers us to choose a different path, one filled with vibrancy and purpose.

Today brought unexpected challenges, but also a reminder of the kindness and support that surrounds us here. Our neighbor Mike, engrossed in his own tasks, generously offered his assistance with a technical issue I faced. His expertise and willingness to lend a hand underscored the strong sense of community we've discovered in Port Isabel.

Melody, my amazing companion, often offers simple yet profound insights that guide me toward a more vibrant and present life. Her words, though unassuming, carry immense wisdom, reminding me to cherish our love and the bonds we share.

'Try to love on your wife
And stay close to your friends
Toast each sundown with wine
Don't let the old man in
Many moons I have lived
My body's weathered and worn
Ask yourself how would you be
If you didn't know the day you were born
When he rides up on his horse
And you feel that cold bitter wind
Look out your window and smile
Don't let the old man in
Look out your window and smile
Don't let the old man in'

And the Winds Came

Wednesday greeted us with abundant sunshine but also gusty winds, the kind that kept Melody mostly indoors for the better part of the day.

With no pressing chores on our agenda and the pool seeming like a distant possibility, we defaulted to our usual routine for such occasions: a circuit of errands that takes us from one stop light to the next, crisscrossing the town to tick off items from our lengthy list.

Our route took us through various stores, including the two resale shops, the liquor store, Dollar Tree, and, of course, Wally World. As my shopping tolerance reached its limit, we headed back on the opposite side, culminating at White Sands restaurant, where serendipity awaited.

Pulling into the parking lot, we found our "next door" neighbors, Terry and Donna, doing the same. We'd often shared our love for this place with them, and tonight, they were here to redeem a discount meal won from a Bingo game.

Seated at a table for four by the water, we watched as the tide ebbed away and the sun dipped below the horizon, a scene too picturesque to capture in a photo. The evening unfolded with delightful conversation and laughter, as we savored both the delicious food and the company of our newfound friends.

As Terry and Donna shared snippets of their life story, it struck us how rare and precious it is to find a lifelong partner. Their enduring bond, forged since high school, stood as a testament to the power of love and commitment.

Reflecting on our own journey, Melody and I recalled the pact we made five years ago when we first met: to "make the best of the rest." We've witnessed firsthand the fragility of life and the fleeting nature of happiness. In the face of such realities, we choose to embrace each day with gratitude and joy, cherishing the profound connection we share.

Despite the winds of life that have come and gone, we remain steadfast in our commitment to making the most of every moment together. For in the end, it's not the challenges we face but the love we cultivate that defines our lives. And as we continue this journey, hand in hand, we're reminded that the best is yet to come.

Lovely Day

Thursday unfolded with the promise of another beautiful day. As the sun peeked over the horizon out my window and bathed the world in its golden light, I found myself filled with a sense of contentment, knowing that with Melody close by, it's bound to be a lovely day.

We spent the morning basking in the warmth of the sun, just the simple pleasure of each other's company. A leisurely lunch of sandwiches and chips only added to the sense of tranquility. With Melody's infectious smile and positivity, I couldn't help but feel grateful for the life we share.

There was a time when my days were clouded by limitations and strife, trapped in a relationship that drained me of joy and vitality. But those days are a distant memory now. With Melody, I've discovered a newfound freedom to be myself, to embrace each moment with enthusiasm, and to savor the beauty of simply being alive.

The lyrics of "Lovely Day" by Bill Withers echoed in my mind as I reflected on the profound impact Melody has had on my life. Her presence is like a ray of sunshine, illuminating even the darkest corners of my heart. With her by my side, I know that no matter what challenges may come my way, everything will be alright.

So, as I look at Melody fast asleep, my heart swells with gratitude and love. In her eyes, I find solace, strength, and the assurance that no matter what the day may bring, it's going to be a lovely day.

'Then I look at you
And the world's alright with me
Just one look at you
And I know it's gonna be
A lovely day'

I Married An Angel

Friday started off wonderfully as we basked in the sunshine at the pool, enjoying the warmth and serenity of the day. However, amidst the splashing and laughter, an unexpected visitor arrived – a kidney stone attack.

As I struggled to exit the pool, feeling the intense pain radiating through my body, Melody rushed to my side, wrapping a towel around me and offering her unwavering support. It was a moment of vulnerability, reminiscent of the lyrics from "*I Married An Angel*," where the strength and care of a loved one become a source of solace during challenging times.

Navigating through the waves of discomfort, I leaned on Melody's steady hand as we made our way back to our tiny home. The agony persisted, leaving me incapacitated and in need of her tender care. With each step, I felt the weight of the ordeal, yet Melody remained by my side, a guiding light in the darkness

The hours that followed were grueling, with waves of nausea and discomfort threatening to overwhelm me. Yet, through it all, Melody's presence was a soothing balm, her compassion and care easing my suffering. In those moments of anguish, she was my angel, offering comfort and reassurance when I needed it most.

As the day wore on and the pain began to subside, I found solace in Melody's loving embrace, grateful for her unwavering support. Together, we weathered the storm, emerging stronger and more united than ever before.

In the evening, as Melody settled in to watch "This is Us," I reflected on the profound impact Melody had on my day. Her sweet, selfless acts of kindness and unwavering devotion were a testament to the depth of her love, reminding me of the lyrics, *"I Married An Angel"*. Indeed, her presence had transformed the day's challenges into moments of grace and gratitude.

'There's been a change in me I have a lovely disposition
That's very strange in me
And life's as sweet as it can be I've lots of courage and
ambition from every care my mind is free
So I repeat with your permission
There's been a change in me'

Born To Be Alive

Saturday dawned as a day of recovery for me, a chance to realign my mind and body after the ordeal of the kidney stone attack. Despite the absence of the sun, I awoke feeling surprisingly well, buoyed by the outpouring of support and well-wishes from friends and followers on social media. Their positive remarks served as a reminder of the resilience of the human spirit and the power of community.

With the day stretching before us, Melody and I ventured out to the Community Arts / Crafts Sale, eager to immerse ourselves in the vibrant atmosphere of handmade crafts and unique treasures. We wandered through the stalls for hours, engaging in conversation with fellow attendees, forging connections, and acquiring a few special items for ourselves and loved ones.

As the afternoon wore on, a sense of tranquility settled over us, punctuated by moments of quiet contemplation. Seeking diversion, we embarked on a trip to Wally World, where the aisles bustled with activity and the checkout lines stretched endlessly. Amidst the chaos, we found ourselves behind a group stocking up for a

Super Bowl extravaganza, their combined 3 carts overflowing with supplies for over $500!

Today's reflection captures a moment of simple contentment—Melody and I seated together in our tiny home, sharing smiles that reflect the joy of being alive. It stands as a testament to overcoming adversity and embracing each day with gratitude and enthusiasm.

In the background, the lyrics of "*Born To Be Alive*" resonate, a celebration of life's vitality and resilience. As the chorus rings out, I am reminded of the innate strength within us all, a reminder that we are indeed born to be alive, to thrive, and to cherish each precious moment.

'*Born, born to be alive (Born to be alive)*
You see, you were born, born, born
(Born to be alive)'

A Paramount Problem

Sunday unfolded under the veil of overcast skies, the thermometer hovering comfortably at 75 degrees. We kicked off the day with a delightful Super Bowl Brunch, a feast that would sustain us throughout the hours ahead. With satisfied appetites, we embraced a leisurely pace, spending the day lounging, indulging in books, and enjoying leisurely strolls with our canine companions.

As the Super Bowl unfolded, excitement filled our tiny home, particularly during that action-packed first half. However, our viewing experience hit a snag when the streaming service, Paramount+ encountered technical difficulties. Despite our best efforts to reconnect, our endeavors proved futile, leaving us to navigate a quiet evening in the company of our furry friends.

In the tranquility of the night, a late-night awakening prompted a brief excursion for a poddy run with the dogs. Curiosity about the game's outcome lingered, leading to a quick inquiry with Siri on my iPhone. The response revealed an unexpected twist in who won.

Sunshine On My Shoulders

Today at the pool, the atmosphere was tranquil, with only a few of us basking in the warmth of the sun. Among us was a gentleman hailing from Kirkwood, MO, whose family roots traced back to North Dakota in the 1920s. Listening to his tales, I couldn't help but marvel at the rich tapestry of history woven into our lives. He shared anecdotes of his days at McDonnell Douglas, where he worked as a buyer for the formidable F-15s, adding another layer to our conversation. I as an intern in their art department drew all the planes produced from 1930's to 1978. Those drawings that I did were turned into etchings in a timeline wrapping around the Museum of McDonnell Douglas on campus in Ferguson, MO.

As we swapped stories and reminisced about home, I couldn't shake the feeling of gratitude for moments like these, where strangers become new friends - as shared experiences bridge the gaps between us. Before our poolside rendezvous, I had the pleasure of catching up with my dear friend, John over the phone. His familiar voice and laughter brought a sense of comfort and nostalgia, reminding me of the value of cherished friendships.

Despite the camaraderie and sunshine, the day wasn't without its challenges. I came back and grappled with lingering discomfort in my left lower back, a reminder of the recent ordeal with kidney stones. Around 5:30 pm, a twinge of pain stirred, and for a moment, I feared the worst. Yet, I clung to hope, praying it was a false alarm. Fortunately, the discomfort subsided after half an hour, easing my worries for the time being.

Though the day unfolded with its share of ups and downs, one thing remained constant—the sunshine. Its gentle warmth on my shoulders brought solace, lifting my spirits amidst life's uncertainties. As I reflect on the day's events, John Denver's timeless lyrics resonate deeply, reminding me that sunshine, in all its forms, has the power to uplift and inspire, casting a golden glow on even the darkest of days.

'Sunshine on my shoulders makes me happy
Sunshine in my eyes can make me cry
Sunshine on the water looks so lovely
Sunshine almost always makes me high'

Long Cool Woman

On this Valentine's Day, I chose the song "Long Cool Woman" to celebrate the remarkable woman in my life, Melody.

Tuesday was truly wonderful, with the sun casting its golden glow and the weather embracing us with its warmth. We spent the day at the pool, where the conversations flowed as effortlessly as the water. Among those we connected with was Marvin, a widower whose tales of adventure filled the air with nostalgia. He regaled us with stories of his journeys across the country, from the tranquil shores of the Florida Keys to the dazzling lights of Las Vegas and the charm of Chattanooga and more. Listening to him, I couldn't help but feel a surge of excitement for the adventures Melody and I have yet to embark on in our tiny home.

As we sat there, surrounded by the serenity of the poolside, I couldn't help but admire the woman in the photo. Melody, in her black spandex, exudes a quiet confidence and grace that captivates me every day. With her genuine presence, she has a way of making every moment unforgettable.

With a long cool woman in a black dress Just a 5'9 beautiful tall

Yeah, with just one look I was a bad mess Cause that long cool woman had it all

In her, I see a reflection of strength, beauty, and unwavering love. Today, as we celebrate love on this special day, I am reminded of how lucky I am to have her by my side. Here's to many more adventures and countless memories with my long cool woman.

'With a long cool woman in a black dress
Just a 5'9" beautiful 'n' tall
Well with just one look I was a bad mess
'Cause that long cool woman had it all
Had it all, had it all, had it all
Had it all, had it all, had it all (she had it all)'

A Memorable Wednesday

Yesterday was yet another delightful day here in Port Isabel, with overcast skies lending a warm ambiance to our adventures. Our main mission for the day was tackling the essential task of shopping. Our journey began at the familiar aisles of H.E.B, but soon we found ourselves drawn to the allure of better prices and a wider selection at Wally World. It turned out to be a wise decision, as we checked off all the items from our extensive shopping list.

And yes, I know that my shopping stamina has its limits, lasting about two hours before I reach my personal threshold. Despite having more places to visit, I was content to call it a day after completing my part of the errands.

The maintenance of our camper occupied our attention as well. Following Monday's power wash of the undercarriage, yesterday saw the application of a new protective coating. With locals warning us about the corrosive effects of salt in this coastal environment, we opted for a recommended solution: 'Fluid Film.' This lanolin-based rust preventive proved to be an effective shield against corrosion, as evidenced by striking before-and-after photos of the treated areas.

After a well-deserved nap, we embarked on a leisurely journey to White Sands for our Valentine's Dinner. Along the way, we made a pit stop at the local RV store to visit Bill. What started as a simple errand to acquire three necessary items turned into an engaging conversation filled with helpful advice and even some suggestions for fun activities.

Yet, the true highlight of our Wednesday was the time spent with Melody during dinner at our favorite, White Sands. It wasn't about the food or drinks (though my shrimp tacos were amazing), but rather the cherished moments of togetherness, celebrating another day, month, and year of shared blessings. In the end, it's these simple joys that truly make life wonderful.

Thank you for accompanying us on our continuing journey!

Count On Me

Thursday dawned with familiar overcast skies in Port Isabel, prompting us to adopt our tried-and-true approach: GSD (get stuff done). Our agenda? A mix of errands, shopping, and a few unexpected surprises along the way. As we embarked on our day, the rhythm of Bruno Mars' "Count on Me" played softly in the background, a reminder of the bonds that sustain us through life's ups and downs.

We began by tackling our shopping list, venturing through local shops and even exploring online options via Amazon to fulfill our needs. However, my personal shopping threshold of two hours soon approached again, signaling it was time to call it a day in that department. Yet, our productivity didn't end there.

A decision was made to address a cosmetic issue with our stove trim, ultimately opting to remove it entirely. The result? A sleeker appearance without the need for any additional purchases or hassle.

Next on our agenda was a visit to the local Marine and Canvas Repair Shop in Laguna Heights to discuss re-upholstering our jackknife couch.

Despite their bustling activity, we managed to secure a slot for next week, armed with fabric samples and measurements. The anticipation of refreshing our living space with marine-worthy material fueled our excitement.

A highlight of the day was our visit to Barking Beauties SPI for Bella's much-needed nail trim (I call her feet talons). The owner's exceptional care and skill with our blind dog left us in awe. Despite previous encounters locally where Bella was deemed problematic, here she found reassurance and gentle encouragement to remain calm throughout the grooming process. It was a testament to the expertise and compassion of the staff.

I also took a few calls to lend a helping hand to two clients in need. One, a long-term partner, sought assistance with integrating and optimizing their MS 365 MX mail server for better performance, while the other, a brand-new client, required guidance on setting up their online presence from scratch. It was fulfilling to share my expertise and see the immediate impact of my assistance, reinforcing the importance of fostering strong relationships and providing valuable support within our professional community.

As the day ended, we reflected on the sense of achievement and the support network that surrounds us. In the symphony of life, each chord played resonates with the assurance that, no matter the challenges we face, we can count on one another to navigate through.

'If you ever find yourself stuck in the middle of the sea
I'll sail the world to find you
If you ever find yourself lost in the dark and you can't see
I'll be the light to guide you'

Raindrops Keep Fallin' On My Head

Friday brought a steady downpour to Port Isabel, but amidst the raindrops, there was a joyful reunion on the horizon. We were thrilled as we made our way to the Harlingen Airport to pick up Melody's brother and wife, Matt and Carol. After a few stops along the way, we safely delivered them to The Palms Hotel on South Padre Island, where they'll be staying for the next few weeks.

As we navigated through the airport, I couldn't help but notice the poignant tribute to the 'Battle of Iwo Jima' and the sacrifices made by our American soldiers. It served as a solemn reminder of the history embedded within this region, once home to a military base that now houses the Marine Military Academy, a prestigious college preparatory institution adjacent to the airport.

With Matt and Carol settled into their accommodations at the hotel, we seized the opportunity to catch up over a leisurely dinner at the hotel's restaurant. The warmth of their company, coupled with the ambiance of the surroundings, made for a special evening. These two remarkable individuals bring an added dimension of joy to our time here, and we eagerly anticipate the adventures that lie ahead in the coming weeks.

Despite the relentless rain outside, our spirits remained undampened. While back home in Collinsville, five inches of snow blanketed the ground, here in Port Isabel, the rain served as a soothing backdrop to our reunion. During the dreary weather, there was a sense of gratitude for the opportunity to share this beautiful place with cherished loved ones.

As the raindrops continued to fall, I found harmony in the lyrics of *"Raindrops Keep Fallin' On My Head."*

'So, I just did me some talking to the sun...
'Cryin's not for me
'Cause I'm never gonna stop the rain by complaining
Because I'm free Nothing's worrying me'

Remember When

Saturday brought winds reaching speeds of 40 miles per hour, causing the closure of the overpass bridge to South Padre Island until late morning. Despite the blustery conditions, our spirits remained high as we eagerly awaited the reopening. Once the bridge was clear, we wasted no time in crossing over to pick up Matt and Carol, embarking on a memorable tour of the island.

With many beach spots shuttered due to the gusty winds, we made the most of our time by exploring various locales. We savored a leisurely lunch at Louie's Backyard and found solace in the company of live music, lingering for hours in its comforting embrace with a singer from Iowa.

Venturing to the other side of the island, we discovered a charming hotel with the inviting ambiance of the 'Quarterdeck Lounge,' where live music beckoned us to dance. As the artist's rendition of Allen Jackson "Remember When" filled the air, we found ourselves swept up in nostalgia and joy.

Our evening culminated in a delightful dinner at The Palms Hotel Restaurant, where we bid farewell to Matt and Carol for the evening. Despite the dreary weather, our time together was nothing short of wonderful.

As we reflect on this day, the lyrics of "Remember When" resonate deeply, reminding us of the beauty in cherishing life's moments, both big and small. For in the years to come, amidst the changes and challenges, we'll look back fondly and remember when.

'Remember when we said when we turned gray
When the children grow up and move away
We won't be sad; we'll be glad for all the life we've had and we'll remember when'

Rawhide

Sunday dawned bright and clear, a stark contrast to the previous day's blustery skies, as we embarked on an unforgettable journey to the 34th Annual Los Fresnos Rodeo (with Pro Rodeo Cowboys) and 44th Annual Cameron County Fair and Livestock Show. With the sun beaming down, we rendezvoused with Matt and Carol, ready to immerse ourselves in the rawhide experience of a lifetime.

Navigating through the thick mud, we shifted into four-wheel drive, determined to conquer the rugged terrain without letting our boots succumb to the sloppiness below. Arriving ahead of schedule, we found ample parking and a sparse crowd, offering us the chance to indulge in fair favorites like corn dogs, hamburgers, and refreshing lemon shake-ups. As the day progressed, Melody satisfied her cravings with chicken wings and fries, all while enjoying the thrilling rodeo action.

Amidst the festivities, we found ourselves drawn to the captivating sights and sounds of the motorcycle show, also a talented band serenaded us with a medley of timeless classics spanning rock and country genres. As the crowd swelled, anticipation mounted, with lines forming for the main event.

Once inside, the atmosphere crackled with excitement as we settled into the stands, eagerly awaiting the spectacle before us. Amidst the sold-out crowd, we witnessed awe-inspiring displays of skill and bravery as cowboys and cowgirls showcased their prowess in a series ofadrenaline-pumping events. From heart-stopping feats of timing and strength to heartwarming moments featuring pint-sized 5-year-old riders navigating goats with hilarious aplomb, every moment was a testament to the enduring spirit of the Wild West in the Rio Grande Valley.

In a stroke of luck, I found myself the proud owner of two drink koozies, earned by successfully lassoing a wooden cow on my first attempt—a fitting memento from a day filled with unforgettable memories. And let's not forget the highlight of the day: Melody's daring adventure atop a live mountain of a massive steer, posing proudly with a 7-foot horn spread—an iconic image to commemorate our Rawhide adventure.

As the sun set on our Rawhide adventure, we couldn't help but feel grateful for the experience, knowing that the bonds forged, and the memories made will be cherished for a lifetime.

'Don't try to understand 'em
Just rope, and throw, and brand 'em
Soon we'll be living high and wide
My heart's calculatin'
My true love will be waitin'
Be waiting at the end of my ride'

Tennessee Whiskey

Monday unfolded into a delightful escapade as we rendezvoused with Matt and Carol at 'Laguna Bob's' on the South Padre Beach, ready to dive into an afternoon filled with lively tunes and good vibes. The air was charged with excitement as two separate bands took the stage one after another, energizing us with their soulful melodies. Amidst the music, we savored a late dinner, relishing every bite as we soaked in the infectious energy of the band and the crowd.

With the sweet rhythm of "Tennessee Whiskey" we found ourselves swept up in the moment, dancing the evening away and immersing ourselves in the camaraderie of newfound friends from across this great country. Each conversation was a testament to the warmth and kindness of strangers, enriching our experience with every exchange.

As the sun dipped below the horizon, casting a golden glow across the landscape, we bid farewell to Laguna Bob's, dropped off Matt and Carol, and embarked on the journey back over the two-mile bridge and into the sunset at Port Isabel. The twilight hues painted the sky in shades of orange and pink, creating a breathtaking backdrop for our reflections on the day's blessings.

During the drive, amidst laughter and conversation, we couldn't help but marvel at the unexpected joys of our extended stay. It was a moment of gratitude for the richness of our lives and the cherished moments shared with loved ones. In the lyrics of "Tennessee Whiskey," we found resonance, a reminder that true love has the power to lift us to new heights and fill our hearts with boundless joy.

As we continue this journey, we carry with us the memories of this Tennessee Whiskey kind of Monday—a day filled with laughter, music, and the sweet embrace of love. And with each passing moment, we are reminded of the immeasurable blessings that surround us, grateful for the precious gift of togetherness. Thank you for sharing our journey.

'I've looked for love in all the same old places
Found the bottom of a bottle's always dry, but when you poured out your heart, I didn't waste it
'Cause there's nothing like your love to get me high'

A Shambala Kind of Day

The day began with a trip to Wally World before the sun had even risen, a mission to gather essentials for the day ahead. As the world stirred awake, I navigated the aisles, picking up coffee creamer for Melody and supplies, including washing and drying the truck - setting the stage for a productive morning ahead.

With tasks completed, I settled into my outdoor office chair with cell phone in hand, the tranquil surroundings providing the perfect backdrop for morning business phone calls and emails. As the day unfolded, I sought solace by the pool, basking in the serenity of the moment and relishing the quietude that surrounded me.

As the afternoon sun reached its zenith, we joined Matt and Carol at Clayton's on the beach, a sprawling oasis nestled along the Texas coast.

Here, amidst the rhythmic lull of waves and the infectious energy of Taco Tuesday, we found ourselves swept up in the melodies of classic rock hits and more, the music washing over us like a gentle breeze.

The beaches stretched endlessly before us, their pristine sands shimmering in the sunlight, while the pier from Clayton's beckoned us to explore its depths. In this moment, it felt as if we had found our own slice of paradise, a place where worries melted away and time seemed to stand still.

As the day ended, we ventured to "Dirty Al's," a local favorite known for its fresh daily catch. Here, amidst the bustling atmosphere and tantalizing aromas, Melody indulged in the delicacy of Red Snapper throats, a culinary delight unique to these coastal shores.

In the fading light of dusk, as the strains of "Shambala" by Three Dog Night echoed in my head, we couldn't help but feel a sense of contentment wash over us. For in this moment, surrounded by good company and the beauty of the beach, we were reminded of life's simple pleasures and the magic of finding our own piece of paradise.

'Everyone is helpful Everyone is kind
On the road to Shambala Everyone is lucky
Everyone is so kind
On the road to Shambala'

The Next 30 Years

Wednesday unfolded before us, a canvas painted with the golden hues of the sun, prompting moments of reflection and contemplation about the road ahead. As Melody and I basked in the warmth of the sunlight, our thoughts drifted towards the next 30 years, a horizon filled with endless possibilities.

It was reminiscent of the day we first met, where conversations flowed freely by the poolside, spanning both the depths of our past and the aspirations for our future. Over dinner, we delved into the failures of our respective journeys—both marked by divorce and the scars of life's battles on our kids. Yet, amidst the shadows, there was a glimmer of hope—a shared desire for a brighter tomorrow.

Melody's triumph over cancer served as a beacon of resilience, a reminder of the strength that resides within us even in the face of adversity. It was during one such conversation that we made a pact to embrace the remainder of our days with unbridled optimism, to seize every moment and find joy in the simple pleasures of life, to 'make the best of the rest'.

Joined by Matt and Carol, kindred spirits on this journey of discovery, we ventured to the Wanna Wanna

Beach Bar for an afternoon of laughter and camaraderie by the shore. The waves whispered secrets of the future, carrying our dreams on their gentle currents as we reveled in the magic of the moment.

From there, our journey led us to bustling venues teeming with life and energy, each stop a testament to the vibrant tapestry of experiences that awaited us. As the day drew to a close, we found ourselves at the Meatball Cafe, breaking bread and sharing stories of future adventures yet to unfold.

In the twilight hours, as the echoes of laughter and conversation filled the air, we couldn't help but feel a sense of anticipation for the years to come. For in the next 30 years, we vowed to embrace each day with open arms, to cherish the bonds of friendship and love that sustain us, and to write a new chapter filled with hope, joy, and endless possibilities. And I hope someday my kids understand this connection between us.

'I think I'll take a moment, celebrate my age
The ending of an era and the turning of a page
Now it's time to focus in on where I go from here
Lord have mercy on my next thirty years'

God Blessed Texas

Thursday arrived with the sun shining warmly overhead, inviting us to embrace the leisurely pace of the day. We rendezvoused on the bayside with Matt and Carol at Laguna Bob's, where the lively tunes of the 'Chrome Wheels Band' provided the perfect soundtrack to our late afternoon. There we indulged in the mouthwatering cheeseburger meal, the flavors danced on our tongues, a testament to the culinary delights of the Lone Star State.

Our adventure continued as we ventured from one hotspot to another, making memories against the backdrop of the setting sun with Melody, Matt and Carol. At the Tequila Sunset Bar, we savored the vibrant atmosphere, soaking in the sights and sounds of the bustling scene until twilight beckoned us onwards.

Our next stop was the Lobo Del Mar Bar and Restaurant, where the stirring strains of bagpipes filled the air at sunset. As the familiar notes of the 'Star Spangled Banner' echoed across the bay, we felt a surge of pride for our beloved Texas, a state steeped in patriotism and rich heritage. The moment was truly unforgettable, a testament to the unwavering spirit that defines the Lone Star State.

In the heart of Texas we found ourselves immersed in the essence of "God Blessed Texas" by Little Texas Band. With each passing moment, we celebrated the patriotism, the beauty of our surroundings and the joy of being together, grateful for the blessings of friendship and the vibrant spirit of the Lone Star State.

'(Cause) God blessed Texas with His own hand
Brought down angels from the promised land
Gave 'em a place where they could dance
If you wanna see heaven, brother, here's your chance
I've been sent to spread the message
God blessed Texas'

A Change Is Gonna Come

Today, we embraced the sweet serenity of doing absolutely nothing. No errands to run, no cooking, no tasks to check off the list—just the gentle embrace of the sun as our constant companion. It was a day of quiet contemplation, a long-awaited respite from the hustle and bustle of pushing the limits in daily life. As Sam Cooke's soulful melody echoed in our minds, we knew that change was on the horizon—a change that we welcomed with open arms.

For a long time, we had been chasing the tailwinds, relentlessly pursuing new daily adventures and experiences in Port Isabel and South Padre Island. But today, we felt the need to pause, to simply be present in the moment and savor the stillness that surrounded us. It was a long time comin', this moment of rest and reflection, and we embraced it wholeheartedly.

Our furry companions, ever faithful and ever present, reveled in the opportunity to join us in our leisurely pursuits. They watched with curious eyes as we lounged in the sun, content to simply be in each other's company.

As the day drifted by in a haze of tranquility, we found solace in the lyrics of "*A Change Is Gonna Come.*" For tomorrow, we knew, would bring new adventures and new challenges as we resumed our pursuit of tailwinds with Matt and Carol by our side. But for now, we basked in the quietude of the present moment, grateful for the opportunity to pause, to reflect, and to prepare for the changes that lay ahead.

'It's been a long
A long time coming, but I know A change gonn'a come
Oh yes, it will'

I Can See Clearly Now

As our Rio Grande Valley journey approaches its 40-day mark, we find ourselves filled with gratitude for the countless individuals who have brightened our path along the way. Each kind thought, comment, and interaction on Facebook has added to the richness of our experience, shaping the narrative of this unforgettable adventure. With each passing day, we compile memories to be cherished, eagerly anticipating the day when we can print them out as a hardback book—a testament to the journey from its inception to our eventual return home in April.

Saturday dawned with the promise of sunshine from sunrise to sunset, the golden rays casting a warm glow over our day ahead. With temperatures hovering around 75 degrees and a cool breeze drifting in from the ocean, we embarked on our journey to South Padre Island, eager to explore more treasures.

Our first stop was the Convention Center Flea Market, a vibrant hub of local vendors showcasing their wares. We wandered through the aisles, soaking in the sights and sounds of the bustling market, reveling in the unique finds and treasures awaiting discovery.

Next, we ventured onward to the northern part of the island, where the allure of the beach beckoned us forward. With a moment of hesitation, we made the decision to forge ahead, navigating across deep sand to the sandy shores in four-wheel drive—a thrilling experience that left us exhilarated and alive with laughter.

At the ocean side Wanna Wanna Beach Bar and Grill once again, we reunited with Matt and Carol, the Dr. Zog Band providing the perfect soundtrack to our afternoon of fun and camaraderie. Amidst the melodies, we found ourselves mingling with other couples, sharing stories and laughter as we embraced the spirit of the island.

As the day ended, our cravings led us to The Meatball Cafe, where the aroma of freshly baked pizza filled the air. With satisfied appetites and hearts full of joy, we bid farewell to another day in paradise, the evening sunset casting a warm glow as we crossed the Queen Isabel Bridge back to Port Isabel.

In the clarity of the moment, we couldn't help but feel grateful for the beauty of this journey and the bonds forged along the way. With each passing day, our vision becomes clearer, illuminating the path forward with hope and possibility.

'It's gonna be a bright (bright)
'Bright (bright) sunshiny day
'Look all around, there's nothing but blue skies
'Look straight ahead, there's nothing but blue skies'

Toes (Zak Brown Band)

It was a picture-perfect Sunday as we made our way to South Padre Island, ready for adventure. With Matt and Carol on board, we headed towards the northern tip of the island, where the Gulf of Mexico's pristine beaches awaited us.

Driving about 10 miles north from the Palms Hotel, our excitement grew with each passing mile. We reached the last entrance, #6 and maneuvered through the soft sand in four-wheel drive until we reached the beach. After parking and setting up our spot, we settled in for what promised to be an unforgettable day.

Despite the chilly waters, the warmth of the sun and sand enveloped us. We spent the afternoon indulging in sandwiches, drinks, and most importantly, each other's company. Stories flowed freely, laughter echoed along the shore, and bonds were strengthened under the azure sky.

As we basked in the beauty of our surroundings, we were treated to an unexpected sight – a group of people riding majestic horses, their silhouettes moving gracefully along the shoreline. Further down the beach, our amazement only grew as we spotted a pack of coyotes, their wild spirits dancing in the fading light.

As the day ended, it was time to bid farewell to our slice of paradise. Departure wasn't without its challenges, with many vehicles getting stuck in the sand ahead of us. Yet, with a combined effort, we managed to navigate through the obstacles unscathed. Thankfully, no accidents occurred, and most everyone made it out safely.

With the sun setting on the horizon, we wrapped -up our day with a satisfying dinner at Tom and Jerry's Restaurant. Reflecting on our beach escapade, we couldn't help but feel grateful for the moments shared and memories made. It was a day filled with adventure, laughter, and the kind of camaraderie that makes life truly special.

'I got my toes in the water, ass in the sand
Not a worry in the world, a cold beer in my hand
Life is good today, life is good today'

9 to 5

Starting off our Monday bright and early, just like Dolly sings, we found ourselves in the 9 am town hall community meeting, catching up on the week's events alongside Terry and a few other familiar faces.

With laundry day upon us, the excitement of the morning meeting quickly faded as we tackled the piles of clothes, bedding, and more. But hey, as Dolly says, "What a way to make a living," right? And once the laundry was done, we welcomed the chance for a well-deserved nap – a little break from the daily sunshine grind.

As the afternoon rolled around, we decided to soak up some sunshine by the poolside, embracing the warmth despite the high winds. Tomorrow holds the promise of adventure as we embark on a boating trip with Matt and Carol, and the anticipation of what's to come keeps us eagerly looking forward, just like Dolly's upbeat tune.

'Workin' 9 to 5
What a way to make livin'
Barely gettin' by
It's all takin' and no givin'

Cheeseburger In Paradise

Tuesday's adventure began with high hopes for a boating excursion alongside Matt and Carol, but as fate would have it, the ocean's waves had other plans, prompting a cancellation. Undeterred, we decided to turn this setback into an opportunity for island exploration, guided all day by the rhythm of "Cheeseburger in Paradise".

With spirits high and a sense of spontaneity in the air, we embarked on an island-hopping journey of a different kind – barhopping, to be precise. Our first stop? Clayton's, where the sun-kissed shores welcomed us with open arms. From there, it was a day filled with culinary delights and tantalizing libations, each stop offering its own unique flavor and charm.

At Laguna Bob's, we couldn't resist indulging in their famed cheeseburgers, perfectly chased by sips of the hilariously named 'Duck Fart' cocktail. As we savored each bite and sip, the infectious energy of the live band TOONZ filled the air, beckoning us to dance and let loose in true island fashion.

Amidst the festivities, I took a moment to appreciate the intricate sand designs outside, each one showcasing the creativity and artistry of the island's visitors. While I can only describe one today, there were more than 15 stunning creations scattered across the area, each a testament to the talent on display.

As the sun dipped below the horizon, casting a golden hue across the sky, our island-hopping excursion came to a serene conclusion at the Upper Deck Lounge. Nestled quietly next to a hotel, this hidden gem offered the perfect retreat to unwind and reflect on the day's adventures, accompanied by the gentle melody of the ocean waves in the distance.

'Cheeseburger in paradise
Medium-rare with mustard'd be nice Heaven on Earth with an onion slice I 'm just a cheeseburger in paradise'

Blowin' in the Wind

Wednesday dawned with a radiant sun, casting an amazing glow upon our morning as we savored a delectable brunch of shrimp and wild rice on the Blackstone grill. The air was filled with anticipation and just the faintest whisper of Bob Dylan's *"Blowin' in the Wind."*

As the day unfolded, I found myself immersed in the task of cleaning the black tank, setting up a menial process to ensure its ongoing working condition. Afterwards, the warmth of the sun soon beckoned me to the poolside, seeking respite from the midday heat.

Yet, just as Dylan's lyrics muse on the unpredictable nature of the wind, gusts began to sweep across the landscape, prompting a hasty retreat to our tiny home. With winds reaching speeds of 30-40 miles per hour, it was a reminder of nature's power and unpredictability.

Securing everything outside, I settled onto the couch with our canine companions, the melody of Dylan's timeless tune still lingering in the air.

Meanwhile, Melody diligently tended to her tasks, updating receipts and accounts with the same steadfast determination as the wind outside.

As the evening approached, we indulged in the simple pleasures of movie night, accompanied by the comforting aroma of freshly popped popcorn drizzled with extra butter. And though our previous plans for that boat excursion with Matt and Carol had been dashed by the tempestuous winds, we remained hopeful for the adventures that Thursday might bring, echoing Dylan's eternal question:

'*How many roads must a man walk down before you call him a man?*
The answer, my friend, is blowin' in the wind
The answer is blowin' in the wind'

I Got Nothin' *(Original by Keith Thorn)*

    Today was another typical Thursday filled with errands and repairs, as I found myself navigating the aisles of Wally World and the RV Store. One particular task awaited me at home - replacing the flush valve seal on the toilet and the black tank tango. It was a job not for the faint of heart, requiring more effort than most would care to admit. However, I tackled it head-on, removing the old seal and installing the new one until the toilet was functioning correctly once more.

    After a day of hard work and successful repair, we decided to treat ourselves to some relaxation at our favorite happy hour spot, White Sands, conveniently located just across the street. As we raised our glasses to another job well done, I couldn't help but reflect on the feeling of satisfaction that comes with overcoming challenges and making things right again.

    Sometimes, despite our best efforts, inspiration eludes us. But in those moments, it's important to celebrate the small victories and appreciate the simple joys that life has to offer. Today may have been filled with mundane tasks and a lack of inspiration, but it was also a day of accomplishment and contentment. And sometimes, that's more than enough.

'I got nothin', just an empty page
Can't find the words, can't turn the page
Tryin' to write a song, but it's all in vain
I got nothin', just this melody in my brain'

Better Together

Friday unfolded as another day filled with errands and tasks, as I set out to tackle various business matters, including making reservations for the winter of 2024-25 for the Port Isabel Park Center Amidst the hustle and bustle, Jack Johnson's soothing melody of "Better Together" echoed softly in my mind, reminding me of the importance of companionship and shared experiences.

In the afternoon, Matt, Carol, Melody, and I embarked on a leisurely excursion, visiting Louie's Backyard for some lighthearted fun. We captured memories with fun photos, grooved to great music, and indulged in appetizing shrimp baskets, all while cherishing the camaraderie that comes with being together.

As the sun began its descent, we ventured over to The Kraken, where we were greeted by the sight of the biggest digital screen I had yet to see indoors. The evening was filled with more live music, creating a harmonious backdrop for shared laughter and conversation.

After dropping off Matt and Carol it was time to tend to the needs of our furry companions. We fed and took the dogs out for a walk, relishing in the simple joys of togetherness, just like the song suggests.

As Matt and Carol's departure loomed on the horizon, slated for Saturday morning, the lyrics of *'Better Together'* resonated deeply. Despite the impending goodbyes, we've loved the memories that we have shared and the bonds that will endure, knowing that true connections are indeed better when experienced together.

'Mmm, it's always better when we're together
Yeah, we'll look at the stars when we're together
Well, it's always better when we're together
Yeah, it's always better when we're together'

Good Riddance (Time of Your Life)

Saturday marked a bittersweet chapter for Melody and me as we bid farewell to Matt and Carol as we took them to the Harlingen Airport and watched them enter the doors for their flight back to Midway Airport, Chicago, where their car was parked for their drive south to Ashkum, the lyrics of Green Day's "Good Riddance (Time of Your Life)" was on my mind.

Matt and Carol's visit to South Padre Island had been nothing short of extraordinary. Their presence brought warmth and joy to every moment, and their departure left a palpable void in our hearts. They epitomize the essence of family and friendship, leaving an indelible mark on everyone they encounter.

Despite the whirlwind of fun and laughter that accompanied their stay, we cherished the moments of much needed rest in between. Like the song suggests, their visit was indeed the "time of our lives," filled with unforgettable memories and cherished experiences, especially driving on the South Padre Island shores in our 4WD truck.

As we look ahead to the future, we find solace in the knowledge that our bond with Matt and Carol transcends distance and time. While we may be saying goodbye for now, we eagerly anticipate the next chapter, filled with more laughter, adventures, and celebrations.

So -- here's to you, Matt and Carol – thank you for the memories, the laughter, and the love and we look forward to celebrating together with fireworks on Lake Shelbyville this coming July 4th, knowing that the best is still yet to come.

As dusk settled in, a thick fog enveloped the landscape with astonishing speed, shrouding everything in an eerie haze. It was a sight to behold, one that seemed to defy the natural order of things. Yet, as the fog descended, it brought with it a sense of mystery and wonder, casting a spell of enchantment over the island. In that fleeting moment, I was reminded of the beauty and unpredictability of nature, a reminder to embrace the unexpected and find magic in the ordinary.

'It's something unpredictable but in the end,
it's right,
I hope you had the time of your life'

True Colors

God knows that in my later journey through life, I've strived to embody kindness, guided by the principles of grace and mercy. Alongside me on this path is my wonderful wife, Melody, whose unwavering belief in the innate goodness and potential of humanity serves as a beacon of light.

Reflecting on my personal history, it's clear that I've encountered my fair share of challenges and setbacks. However, amidst the trials and tribulations, I hold steadfast to the belief and virtues of faith, hope, and love.

Since 1993, I've found solace and discipline in the practice of martial arts, particularly aikido. Through rigorous training, I've learned that mastering physical stress enables one to navigate life's challenges with greater composure. As I impart to my students, cultivating calmness in the face of adversity is key to thriving in all aspects of daily life.

One of the most cherished aspects of our tiny home is Melody's choice to adorn it with the mantra "Be Kind." It serves as a gentle reminder of the power of kindness in shaping our interactions and fostering harmony. In many ways, Melody is the yin to my yang, complementing and balancing our shared journey with her unwavering commitment to spreading kindness and compassion.

As Cyndi Lauper's timeless song "True Colors" reminds us, embracing our true selves and extending kindness to others illuminates the world.

'But I see your true colors
Shining through
I see your true colors
And that's why I love you
So don't be afraid to let them show
Your true colors
True colors are beautiful
Like a rainbow'

Sailing

Our days seem to follow a familiar routine of bustling activity, from running errands to tackling chores, until the sun reaches its zenith, signaling the perfect time for lunch and possibly a leisurely nap in the warmth of the sun.

Amidst the whirlwind of tasks, from crating the dogs to preparing for a poolside escape, our plans took an unexpected turn when we asked to leave the pool area for the oversight of forgetting our wristbands. A quick dash back to retrieve them ensued before we could finally surrender ourselves to the afternoon sun.

As we settled into the pool, Christopher Cross's "Sailing" played softly in the background, setting the scene for a tranquil afternoon on the water. Melody gracefully glided through the pool; her movements reminiscent of a sailboat drifting across calm seas.

Transitioning to the inviting warmth of the hot tub, we found ourselves engaged in lively conversations with fellow pool-goers, exchanging tales of past adventures in Mexico. The shared camaraderie and laughter were akin to navigating the open waters, with each interaction adding depth and color to our collective experience.

In moments like these, amidst the gentle ebb and flow of conversation, we found ourselves truly embracing the spirit of "Sailing" – not just as a physical activity but as a metaphor for the journey of life itself. And as the sun dipped below the horizon, casting a golden glow upon the water, we were reminded of the simple joys of companionship and the beauty of sailing through life's adventures together.

'Sailing
Takes me away to where I've always heard it could be
Just a dream and the wind to carry me and soon
I will be free'

Me & You & a Dog Named Boo

In the serene moments captured by Cardi's peaceful slumber on the couch, I can't help but reflect on the journey she's taken to reach this state of contentment. While "Boo" may not be among the many nasty names I've affectionately called her, it's a reminder of the joy she brings into our lives each day.

From her early days as a nervous young lab mix to the more confident and more attentive companion she's become, Cardi's transformation has been nothing short of remarkable. She's embraced new experiences with enthusiasm, eagerly greeting both furry friends and unfamiliar *hooman* faces alike.

As we watch her blossom in this happy place, our hearts swell with pride and gratitude. Cardi's journey is a testament to the power of patience, love, and the unwavering bond between *hoomans* and their furry companions.

As we look ahead to the adventures yet to come, we're filled with excitement at the prospect of traveling alongside our sweet Cardi for many more years to come. With each passing day, she reminds us of the simple joys of companionship and the profound impact of opening our hearts to love.

'Me and you and a dog named Boo
Traveling and living off the land
Me and you and a dog named Boo
How I love being a free man'

Sweet Potato Pie

As Thursday rolled around in Port Isabel with Melody by my side, the aroma of sizzling food on the Blackstone filled the air, tantalizing our taste buds with the promise of a delicious meal. In the midst of our culinary escapade, I couldn't help but think of Ray Charles and his ode to love in "Sweet Potato Pie."

When it comes to the things we cherish most, food often takes center stage, with potatoes frequently making an appearance in our culinary creations.

Yet, as Ray professed his affection for his sweet potato pie, I couldn't help but draw a parallel to the love I have for Melody.

She's more than just my partner in cooking adventures; she's the sweetest ingredient in the recipe of my life. Like a warm slice of sweet potato pie on a cool autumn evening, Melody brings sweetness, warmth, and comfort to every moment we share together. I am truly blessed.

As we savored the flavors of our meal, with juicy pork steaks, savory mushrooms, and perfectly diced potatoes, I couldn't help but feel grateful for the love and companionship we've cultivated over the years. Melody truly is my sweet potato pie, filling my life with love, joy, and endless warmth.

'Oh lord I feel fine today
I'm walking on cloud nine today I'm over that line today
Happiness is finally mine today
I guess I'm just a lucky guy
And I'm prepared to tell you why
It's strictly on account of my

    [Chorus]

    Sweet potato pie'

At Last (Etta James)

As the evening descended, casting a tranquil blue hue over everything, Melody and I finally indulged in a new experience – slipping into the warmth of the hot tub under the twinkling night sky.

Surrounded by the serene ambiance of the poolside, with the water reflecting the starry heavens above, we found ourselves immersed in a moment of pure bliss.

In the quietude of the night, as Etta James' soulful melody "At Last" came to mind, I couldn't help but feel a profound sense of gratitude. Gratitude for this tranquil moment shared with my beloved, gratitude for the beautiful surroundings enveloping us, and gratitude for the wonderful people we've encountered on our journey.

As I reflect on our time here, I am reminded that gratitude is indeed the key to happiness. It's the thread that weaves through the fabric of our experiences, connecting us to the richness of life and the kindness of others. From the friendly faces of fellow travelers hailing from all corners of the globe – Ontario, Canada; North Dakota, Colorado; Michigan, Minnesota, and beyond – to the stories shared around the poolside, each interaction has been a reminder of the beauty of human connection and the generosity of spirit that abounds in this community.

As we savor these final three weeks in this idyllic setting, I am filled with a profound sense of appreciation for the memories we've created and the friendships we've forged. And as the strains of "At Last" serenade us beneath the starlit sky, I can't help but feel that this moment, this place, and this journey have been nothing short of a dream come true.

'My love has come along
My lonely days are over, and life is like a song
Oh, yeah, yeah'

Rocket Man

As the sun rose over Brownsville, we embarked on a journey that felt like something out of Elton John's *'Rocket Man'*. Our destination: Boca Chica, a remote island area on the road to SpaceX, where excitement hung in the air with a promise of adventure.

As we drove, the lyrics *of 'Rocket Man'* echoed in my mind, adding a soundtrack to our errands in Brownsville and our anticipation of what lay ahead. Boca Chica seemed like a world apart, with its secluded shores meeting the Gulf waters in a dance of isolation and possibility.

Who knew that the SpaceX's campus, the Starship spacecraft and Super Heavy rocket stood as towering symbols of human ingenuity and ambition? These marvels of engineering, collectively known as Starship, promised to carry us not just to Earth orbit, but to the moon, Mars, and beyond. It was a testament to the boundless dreams of exploration that inspired us all.

We eagerly anticipate witnessing the launch scheduled for Thursday morning, feeling a connection to the spirit of discovery that propelled humanity forward. With each passing moment, we were reminded of the words of

'Rocket Man' – "I'm a rocket man, burning out his fuse up here alone" – and the courage it takes to reach for the stars.

Thank you for paying attention to our journey. We'll be sure to keep you all posted as we witness history unfold on Thursday morning. Until then, let's keep dreaming of the endless possibilities that lie beyond the horizon, just like the rocket men and women who dare to explore the unknown.

'Mars ain't the kind of place to raise your kids
In fact, it's cold as hell
And there's no one there to raise them if you did
And all the science, I don't understand
It's just my job five days a week A rocket man
A rocket man'

Peaceful Easy Feeling

As the golden rays of Sunday afternoon spilled over the poolside, we found ourselves enveloped in the serenity of a scene straight out of the Eagles' "Peaceful Easy Feeling." The cool breeze danced with the warm embrace of the sun, creating a perfect harmony of elements that invited us to linger in the moment.

Melody and I cherish these leisurely afternoons spent at the pool and hot tub, where time seems to slow down and worries melt away. Surrounded by the laughter and stories of fellow travelers, we find solace in the simple pleasure of connection and camaraderie. With each passing day, new faces come and go, yet the sense of community and shared experiences remains, grounding us in a sense of belonging.

As the sun begins its descent, casting a gentle glow over the horizon, we reluctantly tear ourselves away from the poolside oasis. But the tranquility doesn't end there. After tending to our furry companions and indulging in a leisurely stroll, we find ourselves at the marina, where the shimmering waters and twinkling lights evoke that same peaceful, easy feeling.

Capturing the essence of the moment, I snapped a few photos, each frame a testament to the beauty and tranquility that surrounds us. And as we stand there, bathed in the soft glow of the evening, I can't help but feel grateful for these moments of serenity and connection, where time stands still, and worries fade away. In the embrace of the evening breeze, we find ourselves at peace, content to simply be in each other's company, with the echoes of the Eagles' melody still lingering in the air.

'And I got a peaceful easy feelin'
And I know you won't let me down
'Cause I'm already standin'
On the ground'

I Can See Clearly Now

As Monday dawned, the community gathered for an early meeting, setting the tone for the week ahead. With activities like the Park Shrimp Boil, Water Aerobics, and Pickleball on the horizon, the calendar buzzed with excitement, much like the upbeat rhythm of Johnny Nash's *'I Can See Clearly Now.'*

Amidst the planning and preparations, Melody carved out time for water aerobics, a refreshing start to the day that mirrored the song's lyrics of newfound clarity and vision.

After a quick lunch, we returned to the pool, where the sunshine danced upon the water, casting its golden glow over the laughter and camaraderie that filled the air. Yet, amidst the joy, there lingered a bittersweet note as we bid farewell to Dan and Gloria from Ontario Canada, who will soon embark on their next adventure this Friday.

Despite the sadness of parting, we embraced the moment, soaking in the warmth of the sun and the warmth of friendship. As the day unfolded, we found ourselves lingering by the poolside, savoring every moment of togetherness and tranquility.

Upon returning home, we began a Blackstone culinary adventure, crafting a delicious entree of chicken, shrimp, and mushrooms infused with onions and spices. The aroma filled the air, reminiscent of the song's promise of a brighter tomorrow.

Before the evening descended, we captured a moment of serenity with Cardi, our faithful companion, her picture-perfect pose capturing the essence of contentment and companionship. In her eyes, we saw reflected the joy of a day well spent, a reminder that amidst life's uncertainties, there is always beauty to be found.

And as we embarked on our evening walk, the echoes of Johnny Nash's melody lingered in our hearts, a reminder that even in moments of change and transition, there is clarity to be found, and new adventures waiting to unfold.

'All of the bad feelings have disappeared
Here is the rainbow I've been prayin' for
It's gonna be a bright (bright), bright (bright)
Sun-shiny day'

Padre Island (Lyndel Lucas)

Today was a whirlwind of activity as we dashed from one errand to the next, seizing the day with gusto. Amidst our bustling schedule, we made a special stop to capture a piece of history – the statue honoring Padre Nicolas Balli on Padre Island.

As we learned more about the island's rich heritage, I couldn't help but be reminded of Lyndel Lucas' soulful ode to Padre Island. In her song, she beautifully encapsulates the essence of this coastal paradise, where seagulls soar against a backdrop of endless blue skies and azure waters.

Padre Island, where time seems to slow down, and worries fade away. With the sand between our toes and the ocean breeze in our hair, we embrace the laid-back rhythm of island life. From the hustle and bustle of winter Texans to the vibrant energy of college crowds and summer vacationers from the Rio Grande Valley, Padre Island is a melting pot of experiences and memories.

As the sun dips below the horizon, casting an amazing glow over the shimmering waters, we find ourselves drawn to the local beach bars, where the sound of crashing waves is complemented by the strumming of an old guitar. With a cold beverage in hand, we savor the simple pleasures of island living, cherishing each moment as it unfolds.

In the lyrics of Lyndel Lucas' song, we find echoes of our own experiences on Padre Island – a place where time stands still, and every day feels like a gift. And as we reflect on the day's adventures, I can't help but feel grateful for the chance to immerse ourselves in the beauty and serenity of this coastal haven.

'Padre island where the seagulls fly
love sand in between my toes no hurry I go with the flow shrimp boats cruising on the water way man I couldn't have a better day cold lone star in a beach bar solo gig and an old guitar'

Dancing in the Street

During the bustling Port Isabel Park Center there's the vibrant energy of Martha and the Vandellas' timeless anthem *'Dancing in the Street'*, there she is – Melody caught in the joyful rhythm of the poolside festivities. As the clock strikes 10am on Wednesday morning, the pool comes alive with people, laughter, and the infectious beat of music, beckoning all to join in the water aerobics.

With each splash and step, Melody immerses herself in the invigorating workout, her smile a testament to the sheer delight of movement and camaraderie. And as the session draws to a close, we refuel with lunch before eagerly returning to the pool for another dose of sunshine and fun.

Underneath the tropical sky, where the temperature hovers at a balmy 83 degrees and the UV index climbs to 8, every moment feels like a celebration of life in this paradise.

As Thursday morning approaches, anticipation mounts for the SpaceX launch, a spectacle that promises to dazzle and inspire. And where better to witness this momentous event than from the comfort of our lounge chairs by the pool, surrounded by friends and fellow adventurers?

In the spirit of *'Dancing in the Street'*, we embrace the invitation to come together, to laugh, to sing, and to revel in the simple joys of life. And as the music plays and the sun sets on another day in paradise, we know that there's always dancing to be found – right here, where the poolside magic never ends.

'It's just an invitation across the nation
A chance for folks to meet
There'll be laughing, singing and music swinging
Dancing in the street'

The Final Countdown

As Thursday morning dawned, our excitement reached a fever pitch in anticipation of the SpaceX rocket launch. However, our pre-launch rituals hit a snag when I stumbled upon a chaotic scene in the kitchen – the Mr. Coffee maker had flooded the pot, leaving nothing but a mess in its wake. In my haste to rectify the situation, I made an even bigger mess attempting to add the lid back on.

Note to self: never try to fix a coffee mishap in the dark.

With the kitchen disaster cleaned up and a fresh pot of coffee brewing, we found ourselves with unexpected time on our hands before the 8:25 launch. Sporting our SpaceX shirts, we dashed outside in the fog to capture the momentous event, armed with cameras to document the morning lift-off amidst the cloud-covered sky.

As the clock ticked down to launch time, the iconic lyrics of "The Final Countdown" by Europe echoed in my mind, adding a soundtrack to the anticipation and excitement of the moment. And then, in a blaze of glory, the rocket soared into the heavens, a testament to human ingenuity and determination.

Despite the obscured view caused by the morning clouds, the sun eventually broke through, casting a golden glow over the scene below. And as we basked in the warmth of the sun and the thrill of the launch, we couldn't help but feel a sense of awe and gratitude for witnessing such a remarkable event.

Indeed, it was the final countdown, a moment we'll cherish forever as we bid farewell to the rocket and its journey into the unknown. And though we'll miss her presence in the sky, we'll carry the memory of this extraordinary experience with us always.

'It's the final countdown
We're leavin' together (the final countdown)
We'll all miss her so
It's the final countdown (final countdown) (Oh)
It's the final countdown Yeah'

You've Got a Friend

Gloria and Daniel, a couple whose warmth and zest for life have left an indelible mark on our time here at Port Isabel Park Center, are the embodiment of friendship and inspiration. Our initial encounter took place amidst the bustling atmosphere of the community Garage Sale, where their Ontario, Canada license plates served as a constant reminder that distance means little when kindred spirits are near.

Their presence, just a stone's throw away from our camper, provided countless opportunities for spontaneous chats – whether in the street, by the hot tub, or lounging poolside. Gloria and Daniel radiate joy and positivity, their laughter echoing through the air as they regale us with tales of family and adventure.

Daniel's boundless energy and infectious enthusiasm were matched only by his willingness to lend a helping hand with any camper-related queries. Our conversations flowed effortlessly, buoyed by his unwavering optimism and unshakeable belief in the power of possibility. In his presence, it was impossible not to feel inspired, and I found myself aspiring to embody his spirit of boundless optimism.

As their time with us drew to a close, we shared a memorable farewell dinner at Louie's Backyard, where the evening's special – a tantalizing half stack of ribs paired with fries and coleslaw – provided the perfect backdrop for our final gathering. Though farewells are never easy, we choose to bid them adieu with a heartfelt "happy trails," knowing that our paths will surely cross again in the future.

As Gloria and Daniel embark on the next leg of their journey, we eagerly anticipate the day when we'll once again be reunited in this vibrant community. Until then, we'll cherish the memories shared and draw strength from the enduring bond of friendship that transcends time and distance.

After all, as James Taylor so beautifully reminds us, "You've got a friend," no matter where life's adventures may lead.

'You just call out my name and you know, wherever I am
I'll come runnin', runnin', yeah, yeah to see you again
Winter, spring, summer or fall all you have to do is call
And I'll be there, yes, I will
You've got a friend
You've got a friend'

Uptown Funk

In crafting this piece, the lively beat of "Uptown Funk" by Bruno Mars might seem unrelated to Chris and Lucy, but its infectious energy mirrors their vibrant personalities.

Chris and his mother Lucy crossed our path back in February here at Port Isabel Park Center, hailing from the heart of Kentucky. Chris, retired Special Operations Veteran, exudes a charisma that belies his age, bringing with him a lifetime of stories and experiences. His love for family and zest for life shine through in every conversation, making him a magnetic presence.

Together, we've shared laughter-filled moments by the pool, engaging in conversations that span the spectrum of topics. And on Saturday night, we took to the town, reveling in the lively atmosphere. Tonight, a stroll down to White Sands restaurant, a favorite haunt of theirs and ours, capped off another memorable day.

Despite the superficial differences, the underlying spirit of "Uptown Funk" resonates with the effervescence that Chris and Lucy bring to every encounter. Their infectious love for family, compassion, and zest for life are a testament to the joy they radiate, making every interaction a celebration.

So, here's to Chris and Lucy, the embodiment of "uptown funk" – vibrant, energetic, and always ready to spread a little joy wherever they go.

'Girls hit your hallelujah (Woo) Girls hit your hallelujah (Woo) Girls hit your hallelujah (Woo)
'Cause uptown funk gon' give it to you (Woo)
('Cause uptown funk gon' give it to you)
'Cause uptown funk gon' give it to you
Saturday night and we in the spot
Don't believe me, just watch'

Don't Stop Believin'

In our latest adventure, Melody and I stepped onto the pickleball court for our inaugural lesson, and what an experience it was! Learning the basics, understanding the rules, and even engaging in a few friendly games ignited a newfound enthusiasm within us – a spark of belief that we could conquer this new challenge.

Guiding us on this journey were Joe and his wife Debbie, the epitome of patience and encouragement. Their unwavering support provided the perfect foundation as we navigated the intricacies of the game, trying to keep our balance, eye on the ball, and spirits high amidst the inevitable self-mistakes.

While my competitive drive grappled with frustrations, Melody embraced the sheer joy of movement and exercise, finding delight in the camaraderie shared by all. With only a few weeks remaining in our time here, we're determined to soak up every moment, absorbing as much knowledge as we can to continue our pickleball journey back home.

Gratitude fills our hearts for the fellow beginners who joined us on this venture, tolerating my occasional outbursts and reminding me to expand my vocabulary beyond four-letter words. And through it all, the timeless refrain of *"Don't Stop Believin"* by Journey echoes in our minds, reminding us that despite the ups and downs, the journey continues – on and on and on.

'*Some'll win, some will lose*
Some are born to sing the blues
Whoa, the movie never ends
It goes on and on and on and on'

What A Wonderful World

As we journeyed through the snow-covered roads in January from Collinsville to Port Isabel Park Center LLC, our arrival was met with a minor setback – our travel trailer's back stabilizers were malfunctioning, leaving me stranded amidst a tangle of wires. It was in this moment of uncertainty that I encountered Mike, and later his wife Ann, two angels in disguise amidst the new January rain.

With his toolbox in tow, Mike graciously lent a helping hand, offering not only his electrical expertise but also his unwavering kindness. Beneath the trailer, amid the debris and chaos, Mike worked tirelessly to diagnose and mend the wiring, a task that seemed insurmountable to me.

As I ventured to the hardware store for parts, Mike continued his diligent efforts, undeterred. Upon my return, I was met with a sight that warmed my heart – Mike had not only completed the repairs but had also resumed work on his own trailer, a testament to his selflessness and generosity.

Amid adversity, Mike and Ann exemplified the beauty and goodness that exists in our world, reminding me of the lyrics of Louis Armstrong's timeless classic, *'What A Wonderful World'*. Their acts of kindness and compassion served as a beacon of hope, illuminating the darkness and reaffirming my belief in the inherent goodness of humanity.

As I gaze upon the skies of blue and clouds of white, I am filled with gratitude for the bright blessed day and the dark sacred night, knowing that amidst life's challenges, look for the angels like Mike and Ann, who make this world a truly wonderful place.

'I see skies of blue and clouds of white
The bright blessed day the dark sacred night
And I think to myself
What a wonderful world'

Footloose

Today's Winter Texan Adventure in Port Isabel calls for the infectious energy of "Footloose" by Kenny Loggins, a song that perfectly embodies the spirit of letting loose and having a blast wherever you are.

At the heart of this lively community is Willie, the Park Manager who never seems to stand still. Whether he's zipping around in a cart or truck, Willie is the driving force behind the smooth operation of the park. With a perpetual smile on his face, he ensures that everyone is having a great time, always ready to lend a helping hand or make decisions with ease.

Assisting management is Angela, the Assistant Manager and Activity Director extraordinaire. Angela's vibrant personality shines through as she orchestrates weekly Zoom meetings, complete with coffee, donuts, and exciting prizes. But it's not all business for Angela – she leads invigorating yoga sessions on Tuesday and Thursday mornings, guiding participants through poses with grace and enthusiasm.

Together, Angela and Willie are a dynamic duo, spreading joy and creating lasting memories for everyone in Port Isabel. With their infectious energy and unwavering dedication, they make every week, month, and year here feel like a treasure trove of unforgettable moments.

So, let's cut loose and kick off our Sunday shoes, just like the lyrics of "Footloose" suggest. With Angela and Willie leading the way, there's no telling where the fun will take us – but one thing's for sure, it'll be a ride to remember!

'So now I gotta cut loose
Footloose
Kick off the Sunday shoes
Please, Louise
Pull me off of my knees
Jack, get back
Come on before we crack
Lose your blues
Everybody cut footloose'

Lean On Me

In the bustling environment of Port Isabel, where new experiences and challenges abound, having reliable support is invaluable. Viola and Rebeca, the dynamic duo of the main office at Port Isabel Park, serve as the cornerstone of assistance and guidance for residents navigating the complexities of daily life.

From deciphering procedures to managing amenities, utilities, and everything in between, Viola and Rebeca effortlessly tackle any challenge that comes their way, turning potential problems into opportunities for resolution. Their warmth, patience, and willingness to lend a helping hand create a welcoming family atmosphere that fosters a sense of belonging for everyone.

Walking into the office and being met with their kind smiles and patient responses to even the most trivial inquiries is a comforting experience. Viola and Rebeca treat each resident with the *"Lean On Me" (Bill Withers)*

In the bustling environment of Port Isabel, where new experiences and challenges abound, having reliable support is invaluable. Viola and Rebeca, the dynamic duo of the main office at Port Isabel Park, serve as the cornerstone of assistance and guidance for residents navigating the complexities of daily life.

'You just call on me brother when you need a hand
We all need somebody to lean on
I just might have a problem that you'll understand
We all need somebody to lean on
Lean on me
When you're not strong
And I'll be your friend
I'll help you carry on...'

Cheeseburger in Paradise

As we strolled through Port Isabel in February, we couldn't help but notice the inviting allure of the 'Burger Shack' tucked next to the Lighthouse. Little did we know, it would soon become our go-to spot for the best cheeseburgers in town!

Melody and I are true connoisseurs of a delicious cheeseburger, and let me tell you, these were absolute perfection. Melody indulged in a half pound of juicy, grilled goodness topped with savory mushrooms and melted Swiss cheese, while I opted for a seasoned half-pounder adorned with tangy blue cheese and mushrooms. With sides of crisp onions and pickles, and a generous serving of piping hot fries, every bite was a taste of paradise.

The ambiance of the 'Burger Shack' added to the experience. Surrounded by quirky signs and nestled amongst artisan shops, it exuded a charm that drew us in from the moment we laid eyes on it. And the best part? The seating options seemed endless, with tables both inside and out, offering plenty of space for diners to enjoy their meals.

As we savored our cheeseburgers in paradise, the lyrics of Jimmy Buffett's iconic song echoed in our minds, reminding us that sometimes, the simple pleasure of a good meal is all we need to feel like we're in paradise. And indeed, with each delicious bite, we felt like we were right where we belonged – in cheeseburger heaven.

'Cheeseburger in paradise
Making the best of every virtue and vice worth every damn bit of sacrifice
To get a cheeseburger in paradise
Get me a cheeseburger in paradise
I'm just a cheeseburger in paradise'

Even The Nights Are Better

In the radiant coastal town, we call home for another 8 days, every moment feels like a dream come true. As the sun graces the sky, we're surrounded by friends like Joe, Debbie, and Gina, daily sharing in the joy of pickleball matches and these sunny pool days, including a sunset trip.

Melody and I are truly grateful for the bond we share with these wonderful people, who make every day in Port Isabel and South Padre Island feel like a treasure. And as Friday night falls upon us, we embark on yet another magical adventure.

Our evening takes us to the tranquil bay side beach, where we dine amidst the gentle breeze and watch as the sun dips below the horizon, painting the sky in hues of gold, orange, and crimson. It's a sight that rivals even the most spectacular of solar eclipses, and we're blessed to witness it together, without the need to wait four years for its return.

On our journey across the bridge and back to Port Isabel, I'm reminded of the beauty that surrounds us each day – the small miracles that fill our lives with wonder. With Melody by my side, every moment can become a cherished memory, and I'm filled with gratitude for this extraordinary adventure we're on.

As the lyrics of Air Supply's timeless song echo in my mind, I realize that indeed, even the nights are better now that we're together. Every day is brighter, every moment more beautiful, since I found you, my love. And as we laugh and talk together on the beach, I'm reminded once again that there's nowhere else, I'd rather be than by your side.

'Even the nights are better
Now that we're here together
Even the nights are better Since I found you, oh
Even the days are brighter
When someone you love's beside ya
Even the nights are better
Since I found you'

Then Came You

Melody and I's journey together began five years ago, and four years ago, we sealed our bond in marriage. What captivates me about Melody is her profound care for her family. She carries their joys and sorrows as if they were her own, demonstrating a depth of love that is truly remarkable.

Melody's passion for literature is as boundless as the stories she adores. One landmark in Port Isabel stands as a testament to her unwavering love for reading—a statue that embodies the essence of her devotion to the written word.

This statue, nestled amidst the charm of Port Isabel, serves as a poignant reminder of Melody's deep connection to books. It symbolizes the countless journeys she's embarked upon through the pages of her favorite novels, the characters she's befriended, and the worlds she's explored within the confines of her imagination.

For Melody, books are not merely objects of leisure, but gateways to enlightenment, solace, and adventure. They have been her companions through every season of life, offering wisdom, comfort, and inspiration in equal measure.

As we pass by this statue, I am reminded of the joy that reading brings to Melody's life and the profound impact it has had on her journey. It is a testament to her insatiable curiosity, her thirst for knowledge, and her unyielding passion for the written word—a love that continues to enrich her life and inspire those around her.

Faith, Hope, and Love are the guiding principles that illuminate Melody's path. While some may falter in finding their faith, Melody's unwavering belief in Christ serves as her anchor. She understands that true faith transcends mere belief, grounding her in a steadfast hope and boundless love.

Though our family members may have made choices we cannot change, we find solace in our happiness together. Despite the disappointment when others fail to see the beauty in our love, we remain steadfast in our commitment to each other.

Melody is the epitome of beauty in my life, and I pray that those close to us come to understand that our past mistakes do not define the depth of our love nor our future. Ever since I met her, she has occupied the deepest recesses of my heart, her presence a constant reminder of the joy and fulfillment she brings into my life.

'Ever since I met ya seems
I can't forgetcha
The thought of you keeps runnin' through the back of my mind
Every time I'm near ya, I get that urge to feel ya
Just touchin' you and lovin' you makes ev'rything right
(tell me how ya feel, baby)'

La Bamba

On this sunny Sunday, our adventure took us to Brownsville, TX, right on the Mexican border, where we dove headfirst into the vibrant energy of the '77 Flea Market'. Spread across a sprawling a square mile it was a bustling hive of activity, offering a treasure trove of goods at negotiable prices.

Melody and I knew that this would be our last Sunday in the Texas Rio Grande Valley for this visit, so we seized the opportunity to immerse ourselves in the endless aisles of vendors, each offering a unique array of items waiting to be discovered.

Sporting my world-famous Shotgun Creek t-shirt, I couldn't help but feel a sense of pride as we explored this bustling marketplace. It might just be the furthest point in Texas, near Mexico, where our beloved band has been represented.

Despite the blustery winds and the dusty air, the atmosphere was electric, with a constant buzz of activity. Parking was akin to navigating a constantly shifting puzzle, with vehicles and people moving about like Mexican jellybeans in a jar.

Much like the iconic song "La Bamba," whose infectious rhythm and energy defy translation, our experience at the flea market was hard to put into words. But as the photos captured moments of laughter, discovery, and joy, we knew that we had embarked on a memorable journey together.

Thank you for continuing to join us on this adventure!

'Para bailar La Bamba Para bailar La Bamba
Se necesita una poca de gracia Una poca de Gracia
Pa' mí, pa' ti, ay arriba, ay arriba Y arriba, y arriba
Por ti seré, por ti seré, por ti seré'

Take A Chance on Me

During our camper's worn-out jack knife couch, which seemed to be on a fast track to decay, we decided to take a chance on a local gem called Canvas Creations right here in Port Isabel. Juan and his mother assured us that they could revamp the terrible, degrading film with marine-grade fabric, promising durability for over two decades. With hopeful hearts, we selected a fabric we adored and settled on a fair price.

Three days later, as I carefully reinstalled the refurbished pieces, we couldn't help but marvel at the transformation. The couch looked utterly stunning and promised to withstand the test of time. With its customizable features, including easily accessible zippers for potential foam replacements, it had truly become a masterpiece. Our gamble on these local artisans had paid off splendidly.

Similarly, our experience with another local craftsman, German RV Repair, echoed our sentiment. His impeccable character, honesty, exceptional skills, and unwavering reliability left us thoroughly impressed. German and his team have come through for us every time!

Reflecting on these experiences, we couldn't help but draw parallels to our own journey. Melody and I had taken a chance on each other years ago, and our shared commitment had enriched our lives immeasurably. Through ups and downs, we've maintained an attitude of gratitude and a steadfast belief in each other, making our journey together truly remarkable.

Some do question the institution of marriage, but we believe that with the right opportunity, the right people, and unwavering passion, taking a chance can lead to extraordinary outcomes.

As the lyrics of ABBA's *"Take A Chance On Me"* resonate in our hearts, we're reminded that love is enduring, even in the face of uncertainty. With a love that's strong enough to weather any storm, we embrace the magic of taking chances and seizing every opportunity for happiness.

'Oh you can take your time baby,
I'm in no hurry, know I'm gonna get you
You don't wanna hurt me, baby don't worry,
I ain't gonna let you
Let me tell you now
My love is strong enough to last when things are rough
It's magic'

Morning Has Broken

As the sun rises in the East and the moon bids farewell in the West, another day begins with the promise of tomorrow when they'll reunite in the sky. Indeed, the morning has broken, illuminating the horizon with a gentle glow, accompanied by the sight of the Aerostat hovering in the distance on the right.

Discovering this unexpected feature in the sky was a delightful surprise for both Melody and me upon our arrival in Port Isabel. Curiosity led us to inquire about it, learning that the coast guard station hosts a blimp for border surveillance purposes. Its presence serves to safeguard the airspace and its surroundings, ensuring safety and security for us all.

U.S. Customs and Border Protection's Aerostat, equipped with a sophisticated surveillance system, plays a crucial role in law enforcement efforts against smuggling, drug trafficking, immigration, and illegal fishing. It stands as a silent guardian, watching over the coastal skies with vigilance. *Interesting facts, huh?*

Moving on, after an invigorating game of pickleball with our friends Joe, Deborah, Bill, Regina, and Lori, we retreated to the pool to soak up the sun's warmth. The day unfolded leisurely, filled with laughter and conversation, as we lounged randomly in the hot tub and embraced the refreshing embrace of the pool.

As the sun began its descent, casting a golden hue over the landscape, hunger stirred within us.

Returning to the comfort of our camper, we indulged in tequila and quesadillas expertly crafted by chef Melody herself.

In the tranquil beauty of the next morning, with birdsong filling the air, we are reminded of the simple joys of life and the blessings of each new day. Like the first morning, with nature's chorus welcoming the dawn, we offer gratitude for the gift of another day, fresh and full of promise.

'Morning has broken like the first morning
Blackbird has spoken like the first bird
Praise for the singing
Praise for the morning
Praise for them springing fresh from the Word'

Peaceful Easy Feeling

Wednesday marked the beginning of our mental transition back home in a few days. As our time here draws nearer, there's a lingering sense of peace and ease in our hearts.

We spent the early day tying up loose ends, running errands, and indulging in some local delights. Lunch at the renowned Burger Shack near the Port Isabel Lighthouse treated us to mouthwatering burgers, followed by a sweet stop at the Davey Jones Ice Cream Locker. The flavors were simply delightful!

Returning to our familiar spot by the pool, we enjoyed the company of good friends like Dave and his wife Carol from Michigan.

Our plans for Thursday morning involve exploring the bustling shopping scene in the Progresso District, where American shoppers find great deals and enjoy the vibrant atmosphere in Mexico.

We're also looking forward to hosting a fun margarita party happy hour at the pool after our Mexico trip.

Here at Port Isabel Park, there's a serene and comfortable atmosphere that lingers. We're savoring every moment, knowing that our time here has been nothing short of blissful.

'Cause I get a peaceful easy feelin'
And I know you won't let me down
'Cause I'm already standin'
I'm already standin'
Yes, I'm already standin' on the ground'

Margaritaville

Thursday dawned with the promise of adventure as we set our sights on Progresso, Mexico, following the lead of our new friends, Bill and Sharon. With their seasoned guidance, we embarked on the hour-long journey, eager to explore the treasures awaiting us in the vibrant streets of the district.

Our morning in Progresso unfolded like a dream, with our first stop at Panchos Bar where we indulged in margaritas and savory enchiladas, setting the tone for a day filled with discovery.

Wandering through the bustling streets, we explored shops and markets, immersing ourselves in the vibrant tapestry of Mexican culture.

Returning to Port Isabel, we reconvened with friends at the pool, where the spirit of Margaritaville awaited. With the help of our trusty Jimmy Buffett Margaritaville machine, we whipped up a round of refreshing cocktails, accompanied by laughter and camaraderie. Special thanks to Dave and Carol for their contributions to the festivities, making our final pool day one to remember!

As the day drew to a close, Jimmy Buffett's lyrics echoed in our minds, capturing the essence of our Mexican escapade and the memories we'll cherish forever.

'I don't know the reason
Stayed up all season
With nothing to show but a brand-new tattoo
But it's a real beauty
A Mexican cutie
How it got here, I haven't a clue, I really don't know'

The Time of My Life

As we bid farewell to Port Isabel, the memories we've gathered here are etched in our hearts forever. Like the lyrics of "*The Time of My Life*" beautifully express, this journey has been nothing short of magical. From lazy days by the pool to unforgettable evenings at the Sands Hotel Restaurant and all the South Padre Island fun spots, every moment has been a treasure.

As I reflect on our time in Port Isabel, I can't help but feel overwhelmed with gratitude for the experiences we've shared. Melody, my dear companion, you've been the shining light guiding me through every adventure. Together, we've laughed, learned, and cherished each day as if it were our last.

Just as the song professes, you're the one thing I can't get enough of, and I'm filled with the certainty that this could be love. Our time here has been a testament to the joy of being together, and I owe it all to you. As we embark on the next chapter of our journey, I carry with me the memories of Port Isabel and the love we've shared, knowing that it will sustain us wherever we go.

'Just remember
You're the one thing I can't get enough of
So I'll tell you something
This could be love, because
I've had the time of my life
No, I never felt this way before
Yes, I swear (yes, I swear), it's the truth
And I owe it all to you'

The Lion Sleeps Tonight

In the early hours of Friday morning, the aroma of freshly brewed coffee filled the air, signaling the start of a new day. With the clock striking 7 o'clock, it was time to attend to the last-minute tasks before embarking on the journey back to Collinsville, IL. As the clock struck 9, we bid farewell to Port Isabel and hit the road along Highway 100.

Our first pit stop was at a fully automated McDonald's kiosk in Los Fresnos, where we encountered some huge delays. Despite the frustration of waiting, we pressed on, now running behind schedule by over an hour and a half. Later we found ourselves at a fork in Highway 39, and unfortunately, Google Maps failed to provide clear guidance, leading us on a detour through central Texas towards Austin and Dallas. Oh, how we wished for clearer directions at the right moments!

As night fell, we arrived at our destination in Texarkana, AK, shrouded in darkness. Though weary from the long drive, we managed to secure a spot for the night without unhitching the trailer. After tending to our immediate needs and those of our furry companions, we settled in for the night, grateful for a safe journey thus far.

For those of you following along on our adventure, rest assured, we made it through the day's challenges. As we retire for the night, the lion sleeps, and we look forward to the next leg of our journey.

'Wee heeheeheehee weeoh aweem away
Rrr, la la la weeoh aweem away
Hush, my darling, don't fear, my darling,
The lion sleeps tonight
Wah oh oh, wah oh oh, wah oh wimoweh
Weeheeheehee dee heeheeheehee weeoh aweem away
Weeheeheehee dee heeheeheehee weeoh aweem away'

Forever Young

Sunday evening brought us back to the familiar sight of our home traveling, with the weary road behind us and the warmth of familiarity welcoming us back. As we stepped out of the vehicle, there stood our neighbors, dear friends who had come to lend a hand and share in our tales of adventure.

Settling into our chairs on the driveway, we exchanged stories of our time in Port Isabel and the journey across the southern landscapes. The laughter and camaraderie eased the exhaustion of the long drive, reminding us of the joy of being surrounded by loved ones.

Now back in the comfort of our own space, we relish in the simple pleasure of relaxation, leaving the unpacking, boatloads of mail, and cleaning for another day. Reflecting on our travels, we are reminded of the importance of gratitude and the value of shared experiences.

As we bid farewell to our travels and embrace the familiar comforts of home, we hold onto the wish for us, and for all our friends to stay forever young. May they find happiness and fulfillment in every step of their journey and may the memories we've shared together remain eternally cherished.

And as we navigate the roads ahead, may the lyrics of *"Forever Young"* by Rod Stewart serves as a guiding light, offering blessings of courage, love, and wisdom for all those we hold dear. Forever young, forever cherished in our hearts.

'May the good Lord be with you
Down every road you roam
And may sunshine and happiness
Surround you when you're far from home
And may you grow to be proud
Dignified and true and do unto others
As you'd have done to you
Be courageous and be brave and in my heart,
   you'll always stay
Forever young, forever young
Forever young, forever young
May good fortune be with you
May your guiding light be strong
Build a stairway to Heaven'

Escape To Port Isabel

Made in the USA
Monee, IL
03 March 2025

31be8c3a-f555-4cfc-8041-2854d5c9129eR01